# SELF-HELP IN AMERICA

*A Social Movement Perspective*

# SOCIAL MOVEMENTS PAST AND PRESENT

## Irwin T. Sanders, Editor

*Abolitionism: A Revolutionary Movement*
by Herbert Aptheker

*The American Communist Movement: Storming Heaven Itself*
by Harvey Klehr and John Earl Haynes

*The American Peace Movement: Ideals and Activism*
by Charles Chatfield

*American Temperance Movements: Cycles of Reform*
by Jack S. Blocker Jr.

*The Antinuclear Movement, Updated Edition*
by Jerome Price

*The Charismatic Movement: Is There a New Pentecost?*
by Margaret Poloma

*The Children's Rights Movement: A History of Advocacy and Protection*
by Joseph M. Hawes

*Civil Rights: The 1960s Freedom Struggle*
by Rhoda Lois Blumberg

*The Conservative Movement, Revised Edition*
by Paul Gottfried

*The Consumer Movement: Guardians of the Marketplace*
by Robert N. Mayer

*Controversy and Coalition: The New Feminist Movement*
by Myra Marx Ferree and Beth B. Hess

*The Creationist Movement in Modern America*
by Raymond A. Eve and Francis B. Harrold

*Family Planning and Population Control: The Challenges of a Successful Movement*
by Kurt W. Back

*The Health Movement: Promoting Fitness in America*
by Michael S. Goldstein

*The Hospice Movement: Easing Death's Pains*
by Cathy Siebold

*Let the People Decide: Neighborhood Organizing in America*
by Robert Fisher

*Populism: The Humane Preference in America, 1890-1900*
by Gene Clanton

*The Prison Reform Movement: Forlorn Hope*
by Larry E. Sullivan

*The Rise of a Gay and Lesbian Movement*
by Barry D. Adam

*Social Movements of the 1960s: Searching for Democracy*
by Stewart Burns

# SELF-HELP IN AMERICA

*A Social Movement Perspective*

*Alfred H. Katz*

Twayne Publishers • New York
Maxwell Macmillan Canada • Toronto
Maxwell Macmillan International • New York  Oxford  Singapore  Sydney

*Self-Help in America: A Social Movement Perspective*
by Alfred H. Katz

Copyright 1993 by Twayne Publishers

Twayne Publishers                      Maxwell Macmillan Canada, Inc.
Macmillan Publishing Company    1200 Eglinton Avenue East
866 Third Avenue                      Suite 200
New York, New York 10022        Don Mills, Ontario M3C 3N1

Macmillan Publishing Company is a part of the Maxwell
Communication Group of Companies.

**Library of Congress Cataloging-in-Publication Data**
Katz, Alfred H. (Alfred Hyman), 1916–
Self-help in America : a social movement perspective / Alfred H. Katz.
    p.   cm. — (Social movements past and present)
Includes bibliographical references and index.
ISBN 0-8057-3877-0 (cloth). — ISBN 0-8057-3878-9 (pbk.)
1. Self-help groups—United States. I. Title. II. Series.
HV547.K369  1993
361.4—dc20                                        92-36285
                                                          CIP

10 9 8 7 6 5 4 3 2 1 (alk. paper)

10 9 8 7 6 5 4 3 2 1 (pbk.: alk. paper)

Printed in the United States of America.

*This work is dedicated to two friends—the late Norman Cousins, exceptional contributor to humanizing medical care, and John R. Seeley, whose polymathic intellectual brilliance and deep human concern I have been privileged to know firsthand.*

# Contents

*Preface*        ix

1. Introduction        1
2. The Two Primary Types of Self-Help Groups        9
3. Common Characteristics of Self-Help Groups        22
4. What Makes Self-Help Groups Work?        32
5. Case Studies of Two Successful Groups        42
6. Leadership, Growth Patterns, and the Role of Ideology        59
7. Relations between Self-Help Groups and Professionals        70
8. Populism and Social Action in Self-Help Groups        82
9. Self-Help Groups and Public Policy        92
10. Self-Help as a Social Movement        103

*Appendix*        111
*Notes*        113
*Bibliography*        120
*Index*        125

# Preface

Self-help groups are here to stay. Hundreds of thousands of them with millions of members are functioning all over the world, and they continue to grow steadily: many more are being created than are dying out or dissolving. Groups for coping with physiological and psychological health problems, family problems, and life transitions; groups for debt management, house building, and job searching; groups for relatives of people who have been sent to wars or have been killed in disasters—these and other collectivities can be found in the current broad panorama of activity we know as self-help. This book seeks to detail why self-help has become so important in modern life—why it is that whenever a few people experience a common special problem, they get together and are motivated to create a self-help group.

The organizing principle to which I have adhered is sketching and comparing the characteristics of today's two major varieties of self-help groups: 12-step and non-12-step. The book also expresses some of my basic convictions about human behavior and motivation, which have been influenced by many years' observation of self-help activities. These are reflected in the chapters that follow, but I would like to state a few here explicitly so that readers will be aware of my philosophical biases.

• Self-help ideas and expressions always reflect and respond to broad social developments and changes. Social class, the distribution of wealth, the position of women, educational levels, attitudes toward minorities, and the degrees of democratization, decentralization, and local autonomy all vary considerably in different societies and strongly affect both the acceptance of self-help groups and the particular forms that self-help takes in them.

• Human behavior reflects a unity of mind and body; processes that occur in one dimension always affect the other. This is as true of purely sociopersonal events—the loss of a loved one, divorce or separation, moving to a new environment, life transitions such as adolescence and retirement—as it is of becoming disabled through illness or accident.

• Included in the human endowment—and conditioned by social experience—is the impulse and need for attachment behavior, cooperation, and altruism. We most fully realize our individual self by going beyond our boundaries through the experience of loving, working with, being concerned about, and helping others.

• Self-realization of our potentials occurs most fully when we achieve autonomy and self-reliance. While some dependency on others is always necessary and important, self-confident, mature independence leads to the healthiest and most satisfying social functioning.

The self-help form of organization has expressed these ideas throughout history and continues to do so today; it is a major instrument for sharing problems and obtaining feedback, which helps us to adapt to stressful life problems. The book's title indicates that I consistently seek to consider whether the diverse manifestations of self-help constitute a social movement. Chapter 10 reviews this issue in detail and states my tentative and qualified conclusions about it and my predictions about self-help's future.

As will be apparent, this work draws on many sources—personal accounts by self-help group members, chronicles and reports of the organizations, research by self-help scholars and other social scientists, and personal observations of self-help activities over more than 30 years. I cannot possibly list the legion of individuals and organizations who have generously given me access to their life experiences and knowledge over the years, but I hope that, regardless of whether they agree with all my statements and conclusions, they will find that my presentation of the dynamic world of self-help groups comprehensively deals with its most important issues. Needless to say, inaccuracies and deficiencies in the book are my fault alone, not those of the many persons who have helped me in writing it.

*Chapter 1*

# Introduction

In the last half of the twentieth century self-help groups have had a dynamic, spectacular rise. Because this century has been so rife with wars, famines, economic depressions, ethnic conflicts, nationalism, and other cataclysmic events, self-help groups have been paid less attention by historians and other scholars and, until quite recently, were little known except to their members. Yet countless numbers of such groups exist all over the world: they have helped millions of people, and they are now beginning to be recognized and accepted by governments, human-services workers, and the public as an important social force and a significant resource for meeting people's needs.

No one knows for sure, but there seems to be agreement that at least 500,000 to 750,000 self-help groups operate in the United States, with at least 10 to 15 million members. In a book published in 1976 I speculated that there were 500,000 groups with up to 7 million members,[1] an estimate based on scattered surveys of the numbers of groups found in different communities and on membership figures of some large self-help organizations, such as Alcoholics Anonymous. The Academy for Educational Development in 1980 estimated a total of 750,000 groups, with 10 to 14 million members.[2] In 1983 The U.S. Department of Health and Human Services projected that there would be 1 million self-help groups by 1990.[3]

These approximations or "guesstimates" are all that is currently available; it is impossible to get accurate figures without a large, comprehensive, and expensive national study, which no agency or research group has been ready or able to undertake.

The rates at which these groups grow and decline are also in question. From experience and observation, scholars believe that self-help groups are forming at a steady rate but that, at the same time, some are fading away, dissolving, or changing their names or functions. Here, fortunately, there is a reliable recent study of all the self-help groups in New Jersey.[4] It shows that the number of groups in that state in 1988 increased 12.3 percent over 1987 figures; at the same time, 3.2 percent of groups in New Jersey dissolved or disappeared, leaving a net annual increase of 8.1 percent. It cannot be claimed that this rate of increase is representative of the United States, but it does seem a reasonable estimation of growth.

It is of related interest to know the kinds of new groups being created. In Chapter 2 I define and discuss in detail the great variety of types and fields of work of self-help groups, but it is clear that groups are created whenever a small number of people feel they have a common need that is not being met by existing organizations and about which they feel they can do something by getting together.

The New Jersey study found that the largest number of new groups formed in 1988 were those to help individuals with mental-health problems; the second largest were for people with acquired immunodeficiency syndrome (AIDS) and their family members; the third largest were for relatives of people discharged from mental hospitals.

The creation of new groups is obviously related to social conditions. As new social problems emerge that affect particular groups or classes of people but are apparently not being taken care of in other ways, new self-help organizations are to be expected. Not only the diagnosis or discovery of new diseases such as AIDS leads to the formation of new groups, but also such massive social problems as addiction to various drugs, child abuse and other forms of family violence, chronic gambling, overeating, the emotional strain of divorce on children, unemployment, and sociopolitical events that directly affect the individual, such as the 1991 Gulf War, have all led to the creation and growth of new groups. That this marked trend will continue into the twenty-first century seems a safe prediction.

Everything that has been said about self-help groups in the United States applies as well to other countries, especially industrialized ones. In Great Britain, Germany, the Netherlands, Belgium, and the Scandinavian countries groups are found in substantial numbers, although there are fewer overall than in the United States. In the former Eastern-bloc countries a few groups have formed since about 1960, and there are signs of recent increases, especially groups for people with physical illnesses, children with handicaps, and alcoholics.

In the Third World countries of Africa, Southeast Asia, and Central and South America self-help takes a different form. The most pressing social concerns in these countries are the economy, food supply, sanitation and other environmental and public-health problems, education, and technological development. The gravity of these concerns leaves little room for attention to problems of personal adjustment to illness, stress, and social maladaptation. But self-help activities—often arising from and related to cultural, tribal, and religious customs—exist widely in these societies and are frequently used to solve a basic common problem: securing a safe water supply or an irrigation system for a village.

All indications point to the fact that self-help groups are found in most countries of the world. Despite great differences in culture, social and economic development, and life-styles, many of the modern problems are universal, and the self-help response to them seems universal also.

## The Origins of Self-Help in England

Probably the first and best-known—certainly the most influential—writer about self-help was the Russian aristocrat and anarchist Peter Kropotkin. In his masterwork, *Mutual Aid: A Factor in Evolution* (1939), Kropotkin analyzed animal and human societies and concluded that mutual aid (a synonym for self-help) and cooperation, rather than mutual struggle and predation, enabled societies to survive and develop. He wrote, "The species in which individual struggle has been reduced to its narrowest limit and the practice of mutual aid had attained the greatest development are invariably the most numerous, the most prosperous and the most open to further progress. . . . *In the ethical progress of man, mutual support—not mutual struggle—has had the leading part.*"[5]

Kropotkin was thus arguing against what at the end of the nineteenth century was known as Social Darwinism—the mechanistic extension to human societies of Darwin's theory of evolution and the principle of the "survival of the fittest." Kropotkin showed that tribal or clan societies that survived the rigors of the environment did so because they had customs and laws that supported cooperative action. Early habits of cooperative food gathering and group defense resulted in the establishment of a new type of social organization, the village community, while noncooperating clans were weaker, disintegrated, or were captured. More recent anthropological studies confirm Kropotkin's thesis—common interest, mutual-aid groups appeared early in human society, were widespread, and fostered survival.

These groups arose to defend communities against a common enemy or oppressor; to give material aid and emotional support to individuals and families when disasters occurred; to preserve a religious or cultural belief, tradition or skill in the face of opposing social pressures. Many religious brotherhoods, guilds, and secret societies like the Masons were formed during the Middle Ages to defend members against political or religious persecution and discrimination. The demise of feudalism brought large numbers of peasants to the cities of Europe, where their destitution, hunger, and lack of occupational skills resulted in privation and misery, epidemics like the Black Death, and social upheavals that lasted for decades.

In England social unrest was temporarily stabilized by the passage of the harsh Poor Laws of 1601, which were imported to colonial America and became the foundation of our present welfare system. As England's population grew and the effects of the Industrial Revolution in its cities and the agricultural revolution in its hinterlands became evident, social, economic, and health problems expanded chaotically, and neither government nor the traditional church charities could meet the resultant needs. (In many ways this period parallels the situation in which the United States found itself from 1930 to about 1934.)

English commoners devised three major ways of coping with these problems, all of which embodied self-help or mutual-aid principles: trade unions, "Friendly Societies," and consumer-producer cooperatives.

**Trade Unions** The forerunners of trade unions were artisans who, feeling threatened by the establishment of mechanized factories, organized local trade clubs for common defense. One such group was the Leicestershire woolcombers, about whom an observer wrote in 1761,

> Their first pretence was to take care of their poor brethren that should fall sick, or be out of work . . . and when they became a little formidable they gave laws to their masters, as also to themselves—viz. that no man should comb wool under 2s., per dozen; that no master should employ any comber who was not of their club; if he did they agree one and all not to work for him . . . and often times would abuse the honest man that would labor; they further support one another in so much that they are become one of society throughout the kingdom. And that they may keep up their price to

encourage idleness rather than labour, if anyone of their club is out of work, they give him a ticket and money to seek for work at the next town where a box club is, where he is also subsisted; by which means he can travel the kingdom round, be caressed at each club, and not spending a farthing of his own or strike one stroke of work.[6]

By the end of the eighteenth century such clubs existed among hatters, brushmakers, coopers, cotton-spinners, sailmakers, brick-layers, silk-weavers, carpenters, printers, and many other skilled trades. In addition to their self-help activities for members, these clubs sought, namely by appeals to Parliament, to protect wage standards and apprenticeship arrangements from the effects of unlimited competition.

These groups' activities—to increase wages and improve safety in the workplace—were greatly opposed by employers, who moved Parliament to pass the Combination Acts of 1799 and 1800, under which all unions were considered associations in restraint of trade and were declared illegal. Strikes were prohibited, but enforcement was lax, and the Combination Acts were repealed in 1824.

**Friendly Societies**  Friendly Societies grew out of the late-medieval guilds, which were organizations of skilled workers who had a common trade, such as dyers, goldsmiths, carpenters, and gardeners. Some guild members were excluded from Poor-Law relief because they were aliens; some individual trades went into decline because of the unavailability of import materials. Friendly Societies helped their members by providing money and food in times of sickness in the family, by subsidizing burials, and by making available loans and other services. By the end of the eighteenth century some 200 Friendly Societies existed in Great Britain, with a total membership of 648,000; by 1815 there were at least 400 such groups, with 925,000 members (Thompson, 213).

Structurally, Friendly Societies were self-governing, locally organized bodies that had strict rules for carrying out their purposes and conducting meetings. In addition to providing loans for the needy, insurance for the sick, and burial tasks, they organized club nights, outings, picnics, and holiday celebrations for their members. Their preambles stressed Christian charity, social brotherhood, and the continual need for mutual assistance and support. The noted English historian E. P. Thompson wrote of their effects, "Every kind of witness in the first half of the 19th century—clergymen, factory inspectors, Radical publicists, remarked upon the extent of mutual aid in the poorest districts. In times of emergency, unemployment, strikes, sickness, childbirth, then it was the poor 'who helped everyone his neighbor'" (6).

Friendly Societies were still important in Great Britain even in more modern times: by 1900 there were 17,000 of them and still as many as 18,000 in 1945, when the British Social Security program was greatly improved. Their services in this century included housing and building help, workmen's compensation, insurance loans for farm animals and equipment, and trading activities.

**Cooperatives**   Also arising primarily from the Industrial Revolution in England (although a few similar examples have been documented earlier in Europe) were local cooperative organizations to buy and sell food and other products advantageously. Their self-help activity was limited to the economic sphere: they did not provide the range of personal services and social interactions of Friendly Societies but obviously met important needs. The best-known cooperative was the Rochdale Society (named after its city of origin), where weavers, shoemakers, and other craftsmen jointly bought work materials and consumer goods.

In 1862 some 440 cooperative societies based on the Rochdale model were registered in England and Wales, with a membership of 90,000; by 1890 the number had increased to 1,300, with more than 900,000 members.[7] English cooperative groups had considerable influence on Europe—particularly Russia, France, and Denmark—in the nineteenth century, and this influence spread to Canada and the United States in the twentieth.

## Self-Help in the United States

Mutual aid was practiced by American colonists because in small communities neighborliness was necessary for crop planting and harvesting, for house building, and for protection against hostile native Americans and other settlers. But the fertility and availability of land and the absence of centralized, oppressive state controls made mutual aid less necessary here than in England and Europe, and the American ethos of making it through individual effort alone soon took over.

Of course there were some exceptions: dairy cooperatives in the East, irrigation cooperatives among the Mormons in Utah, and a number of short-lived "utopian" cooperative villages—such as Brook Farm in Massachusetts—to which people could escape from the crowded, unsanitary cities.

The major form of self-help in nineteenth-century America, however, was found in the trade unions, which performed many services of a mutual-aid nature. In addition to collective bargaining about wages and working conditions, the unions were concerned with other ways of improving the personal lives of their members. The Knights of Labor, the first national trade union in the United States, supported consumer cooperatives; many unions developed health insurance, pension plans, banks, credit unions, and cooperative housing projects. In times of unemployment and strikes, unions gave financial assistance to members and their families, and they were also important in organizing social events for members and their families, including summer camps for children.[8]

**Immigration and the Ethnic Dimension** A distinct variety of self-help was created by and for the immigrants who began to arrive in the United States in large numbers at the time of the Irish potato famine in the 1840s. By 1880 there were massive waves of immigrants from Southern, Central, and Eastern Europe. Evidence suggests that many immigrants turned to one another for help soon after arrival. Their problems were many. Whether they lived in the crowded cities or in isolated rural communities, the newcomers had to eke out a living while learning a new language. At the same time, they were met with hostility or lack of understanding by much of the population—by the press, by schools, by the courts and police, and by social-service and charitable organizations.

To counter these difficulties, immigrant groups organized networks for self-help and mutual aid, based on the country, region, or even the town they came from. Benefits of all kinds were provided—new arrivals were met at the dock, given temporary housing if they had no place to stay, and later helped to find work. Sometimes they were given interest-free loans to start small businesses. English-language and other educational classes were often organized for the newcomers. Sickness and death benefits, burial assistance, and sisterhoods and brotherhoods for visiting the sick were often provided.[9]

By the period between the two World Wars these previously important self-help and mutual-aid fraternal organizations became less vital, since the earlier immigrants had been largely assimilated and European immigration had slowed to a trickle. The value of the self-help organizational form and the services it offered have remained clear, however: since

World War II new immigrant groups from Southeast Asia, Central and South America, parts of Africa, the Middle East, and the former Soviet Union have all brought with them or formed self-help groups soon after arrival; these groups perform functions similar to those of earlier times.

**The Current Scene**  The decades after World War II saw the rise of the modern self-help movement in the United States and elsewhere in the world. The war and ensuing social movements and crises of the 1950s and 1960s—the civil rights struggles, the Vietnam War, the War on Poverty, the "counterculture," the women's movement—overshadowed the painstaking creation of groups for mutual support and aid by many needy, socially stigmatized, disenfranchised, and like-minded people throughout the country.

After the granddaddy of self-help organizations, Alcoholics Anonymous, was founded in the mid-1930s, groups dealing with children physically or emotionally ill or with handicaps were the first to surface, most in the post–World War II years. These were quickly followed by myriad special-purpose self-help groups, whose proliferation seemed to reach a crescendo in the late 1960s, has continued throughout the 1970s and 1980s, and gives no signs of a slackening or dying out.

Thus, this book takes a look at the current self-help scene: what these groups are like, how they have developed in some unique ways, and what they do for people. Subsequent chapters review information on their current numbers and types, analyze the reasons for their dramatic rise since about 1950, examine the great variety of their different forms and functions, consider their similarities and differences from professional forms of helping, and speculate about their future as a social movement.

*Chapter 2*

# The Two Primary Types
# of Self-Help Groups

The great diversity of today's self-help groups is reflected in a 1988 directory that describes more than 500 separate national, statewide, regional, and local groups and about 25 self-help clearinghouses.[1] Its index includes almost 300 headings for problems for which more than one self-help group exists: examples are Adult Children of Alcoholics, Depression after Delivery, 40+ Club, Fundamentalists Anonymous, Mothers of AIDS Patients, Premenstrual Syndrome, Spouses of Firemen, Tough Love, Women Who Love Too Much, and Workaholics Anonymous.

Self-help groups can be classified according to, among other ways, the subjects they deal with; who started them; specific ethnic, sex, or age groups they target; and whether they believe and engage in actions to change social policies. (The most comprehensive and up-to-date of the many classification schemes is found in Katz and Bender's 1990 book *Helping One Another: Self-Help Groups in a Changing World* [see the Appendix].) The most fundamental and important classifying distinctions among current self-help groups are, however, whether the group is a so-called 12-step group or a non-12-step group.

## 12-Step Groups

Alcoholics Anonymous is the prototype of all 12-step self-help groups; it is the oldest and has by far the largest number of members and local units in the United States and other countries. Its success has prompted the formation of a host of other self-help organizations that deal with addictions, and it has powerfully influenced these groups' philosophies and operating procedures. Overeaters Anonymous (founded in 1965), Gamblers Anonymous (founded in 1970), Narcotics Anonymous (founded in 1953), and, more recently (1979), Cocaine Anonymous are among the best-known groups that have modeled themselves on A.A. and use the methods it pioneered. Many, though not all, of the 12-step groups use the word *Anonymous* in their names; others use the word in their names to denote that they protect the confidentiality of their members but otherwise do not follow the 12-step approach and methods. Parents Anonymous, a group for parents who abuse their children, and Emotions Anonymous, are examples.

A.A.'s history is fairly well known even outside the self-help field. The group was started in 1935 by two chronic alcoholics, a New York stockbroker and an Ohio surgeon, both of whom had unsuccessfully been trying to stop drinking for years. The stockbroker had had a spiritual experience, stimulated by the English Oxford Group, a Protestant movement that emphasized personal redemption through verbal honesty, admission of defects, reparations to others for past wrongs, and belief in God. The stockbroker realized that to save himself from drinking he must carry a similar message and program to, and be supported by, other alcoholics. He and the surgeon began to work with alcoholics in an Akron, Ohio, hospital, and by the end of 1935 the first A.A. group had been formed. As the basic ideas of A.A. spread, groups arose in several cities; they considered themselves part of the Oxford Group. In 1938, however, the book *Alcoholics Anonymous*, written by the group's two founders, was published, and an independent organization was created with that name to bring together the scattered local groups.

Basic to the founders' initiative to create self-help support groups for personal redemption were their feelings of hopelessness and despair: they had touched rock bottom, they could not make it on their own, and "professional" help did not supply the answers. Because nothing else worked, they came together to find support and help from each other. *Alcoholics Anonymous,* the movement's "Big Book" now in its third edition, documents these feelings in many personal case histories of people who had touched bottom. In a different field of addiction, a chronic gambler vividly expresses being in a similar state:

> I was in hock up to my ears, I had lost all my self-respect. I couldn't look
> anybody in the face. . . . I was always trying for the big score . . . and the

harder I tried, the more I kept getting in deeper and deeper. Any what the hell was the big score anyway? I made it a couple of times so what did I do with it? I blew it . . . my wife never even got a dress or a pair of shoes out of it. . . . *But you know the routine as well as I do, we're all the same, we've all gone the same route.* But things are different now since I've joined GA.[2]

The history of A.A. reveals that the kind of treatment alcoholics needed was hardly ever available from established medical or mental-health professionals. At the time of A.A.'s founding and since, psychiatrists and psychologists have had a discouraging record in treating problem drinkers. This has also been the case for persons with other addictions—chemical, physiological, and psychological. Chronic drug dependency or such behavior as compulsive gambling, overeating, or spouse abuse were not handled with conspicuous success by physicians and mental-health professionals. Whatever the reasons for these professional failures, the founders of 12-step groups and people who joined them had come to realize that conventional approaches to their problems were not helpful. A.A.'s success and dynamic growth provided a role model and a ready-made philosophy and methodology for dealing with similar problems. As of 1992 there are at least 130 national 12-step organizations and a host of statewide and unaffiliated local ones.

As a guide to the psychological changes A.A.'s founders sought to achieve in themselves and other alcoholics, they formulated a program of "12 steps" that they considered a developmental process each member had to undergo to stop drinking. A.A.'s 12 steps (as follows) have given this type of self-help group its popular name, and the many organizations that have modeled themselves on the A.A. format use these steps with minor modifications.

1. We admitted we were powerless over alcohol—that our lives had become unmanageable.
2. Came to believe that a Power greater than ourselves could restore us to sanity.
3. Made a decision to turn our will and our lives over to the care of God as we understood Him.
4. Made a searching and fearless moral inventory of ourselves.
5. Admitted to God, to ourselves, and to another human being the exact nature of our wrongs.
6. Were entirely ready to have God remove all these defects of character.
7. Humbly asked Him to remove our shortcomings.

8. Made a list of all persons we had harmed, and became willing to make amends to them all.

9. Made direct amends to such people wherever possible, except when to do so would injure them or others.

10. Continued to take personal inventory and when we were wrong promptly admitted it.

11. Sought through prayer and meditation to improve our conscious contact with God as we understood him, praying only for knowledge of His will for us and the power to carry that out.

12. Having had a spiritual awakening as the result of these steps, we tried to carry this message to alcoholics, and to practice these principles in all our affairs.[3]

All new members are expected to accept and to progress through these steps at their own pace (there is no time limit or schedule) and with the help of others, gained at and between meetings, and by reading books and other A.A. materials. Members may take years to complete the steps, and if they get stalled or regress, this is understood and accepted.

**Meetings**   Meetings customarily begin with a reading of the "Prayer of Serenity," which is sometimes followed by a formal statement defining the group and its goals. The leader then asks if there are any new members present. New members raise their hands, state their first names, and the group in unison greets each newcomer with "Hi, [name], welcome."

Different members might then read from some basic materials, such as the 12 steps or 12 traditions—statements of A.A. principles and organizational policies set up to guide individual member behavior and local unit operators. This section can occupy up to one-third of the meeting time. The readings often have spiritual significance, perhaps referring to "a will beyond ourselves" or a "Higher Power" or emphasizing the value of prayer. Next, a veteran group member or an experienced person from another unit might deliver a speech. These speeches are usually personal and autobiographical, with an inspirational purpose and message.

Then comes what for many 12-steppers is the most important part of the meeting—the "pitches." Anyone who wants to talk about a personal event, significant article or passage they have read, or anything else, raises a hand and is called on by the leader. Some meetings strictly limit the pitches to three or five minutes; others do not. Aside from the greetings in unison to newcomers, this is the part of the meeting that encourages participation: members await their chance to pitch and are gratified by doing so. Before or after the pitches some form of recognition is given to people who have remained clean of the addiction—for a week, a month, several months, or more. For longer anniversaries—one year, five years, 10 years—a "birthday" cake or other gift may be presented. The meeting concludes with announcements, coffee, and general socializing.

While the preceding depicts a typical 12-step meeting format and some of the elements described are always found, meetings vary considerably according to the individual chapter or unit. The amount of time devoted to readings from the "good books," to an inspirational speaker, and especially to pitches varies greatly. This flexibility stems from the lack of centralization and control in 12-step groups, one of A.A.'s 12 traditions. In some Overeaters Anonymous and A.A. meetings the more common procedural steps, including prayers, readings, and speakers, may be omitted and the meeting devoted exclusively to pitches, or what many members refer to as "dumping," when members speak about their difficulties and frustrations in following the 12-step program.

Contemporary 12-step groups vary widely in the degree to which spirituality is emphasized: at some meetings references to a Higher Power are seldom heard, except when quoting the 12 steps. These chapters or units may accept agnostics or atheists as members, as long as they are ready to accept the other tenets and strive to follow the program for personal change. In the last few years, though, several groups have been set up by former A.A. members specifically to provide the program for nonbelievers. Among them are Rational Recovery Systems and Secular Organization for Sobriety, both founded in 1986.

The diversity in meeting format of and in the general tone and climate of individual units makes it possible for 12-step members in larger cities to sample and shop around until they find the unit most congenial to their needs. For example, a Hollywood A.A. group founded by entertainment industry people and calling itself "Architects of Adversity" meets each weekday at noon, and, as reported by participants, the 1.5-hour meetings are exclusively devoted to dumping.

The 12-step groups are a prominent, much-publicized segment of the self-help movement; because of the dramatic kinds of problems they deal with, they seem especially newsworthy. There has been a lot of recent pro-and-con discussion in the media about a new 12-step organization, Co-Dependents Anonymous, for people who give too much of themselves to looking after a relative or friend addicted to alcohol or other drugs. Co-dependency of this kind is said to be widespread, and self-help groups to help overcome it are growing fast, but CDA has been strongly criticized for advocating "selfish" indifference to others' problems.

## Non-12-Step Groups

While A.A. and its derivatives were developing, a large number of self-help groups were being created in the United States to meet other kinds of needs. Among the earliest of these were groups formed by parents of children with serious illnesses or handicapping conditions—conditions that the parents felt were not well-understood and dealt with by existing professional services. Although there were a few scattered local precursors, parent-organized groups began to surface in a big way in the late 1940s. Organizations to help parents care for children with such chronic diseases or conditions as mental retardation, cerebral palsy, hemophilia, and muscular dystrophy were in place by the early 1950s. Spontaneously formed local groups of parents sought each other out and coalesced into state and national organizations by the early 1950s, which saw the establishment of the Association for Retarded Children and the National Hemophilia Foundation. These groups did much to publicize the problems they dealt with, to encourage professionals to pay more attention to them, and to influence government. When President John F. Kennedy set up a commission to study services for the mentally ill and retarded in 1962, he singled out the Association for Retarded Children as the most influential force in calling public attention to the plight of these Americans.

Thirty years later parent-organized self-help groups to help ill and disabled children are still being created at a steady rate. This firsthand account of the formation of one such group was given in 1990:

PARENTS FOR PARENTS was established ten years ago, in March, 1980. Like most self-help groups, it was created out of personal need. Eleven years ago this February 28th, my son and first child, Andrew, was born with a genetic intestinal disorder called Hirschsprung's Disease. At that time, I was devastated and feeling very alone, as if I was the only parent facing the illness of a child. What I learned, was that I was not alone, and that there was a very special bond between parents of children with any type of medical problem. The bond existed naturally, at the hospital, but ended when the parent and child went home. Parents For Parents was established to bridge the gap between the natural support at the hospital and the need for long term support at home. It also addresses the need for parents to find others whose children are facing a similar medical problem.

The primary service of Parents for Parents is a telephone network that refers parents on the basis of their child's illness. In addition to that, we host three monthly meetings at different hospitals, in the New York metropolitan area. We are somewhat unique in that we offer emotional support and practical information to any parent whose child is facing any type of medical problem, rather than specializing in one particular illness. As a result, we have a large referral list that spans many common and rare illnesses as well.[4]

People form non-12-step groups not only to aid their children but to deal with other personal stresses—illness, bereavement, marital problems, divorce, retirement, or looking after a sick relative. One of the founders of SHARE, a group for women who have had a mastectomy, describes her motivations and experiences:

Fourteen years ago, when I discovered a lump on my breast, I never would have believed that anything good could have evolved from that experience. The diagnosis of cancer is devastating; it can signify disability, deterioration, pain and death. Dealing with permanent uncertainty as to how to cope with this disease and its outcome, and learning to integrate it into your normal life requires a great deal of support. I found my support in SHARE. In August 1976, a concerned physician, Dr. Eugene Thiessen, initiated a support group for women with breast cancer. There were 15 women present besides myself at that first meeting, and we all came together in an era when cancer was still "in the closet," and we felt a great deal of shame in admitting to the world that we had it, because *that* word, cancer, signified death.

Our support group started, and we discussed our fear, and depression, and often anger at the physician, and our altered perception of ourselves, particularly physical, since mastectomies were the order of the day. Some of us were fearful of loss of employment if our disease became public. We discussed whom to tell, when to tell, and how to handle dating and sexual issues. We cried together, we laughed together, and we began to feel less isolated and alone. We gathered strength from each other, and read everything we could about the newest research in breast cancer. We developed the conviction that we had the right to control our own bodies, and be involved in decision-making with our doctors. We worried about every ache and pain, and laughed with relief when an ache in our foot was merely a corn and not cancer. We began to re-establish priorities, and take one day at a time. We found that mourning and grieving were appropriate and had to take their natural course, so that these feelings would not go underground and sabotage other areas of our lives. We became more tolerant of other approaches, and learned to listen when that was all we could do.[5]

Another cancer patient who founded a self-help group describes similar experiences and feelings:

In 1980 when I was diagnosed with cancer, there were no opportunities to talk with others who had cancer. The possibility was not suggested, and I did not ask about it. Even if I had asked, there would have been nowhere to turn in my home town for that kind of service. One year after diagnosis I began seeing a counselor. Many of my initial reasons for entering therapy were questions about the way I was handling my cancer experience. Was I crazy? Why wasn't I able to get on with my life and forget about the cancer? I found myself alone in my experience and having difficulty dealing with the reality of life after cancer. There were 20,000 fellow cancer survivors in New Mexico, over 8,000 in the Albuquerque area where I lived, yet I was feeling alone and isolated.

Professional counseling was helpful, but it was not until I attended an educational forum set up by an oncologist and there began talking with others who had cancer that I really began to find answers to my questions. Talking with others who had cancer also relieved the heavy feelings of isolation and victimization that I had carried during and after my cancer experience. In fact, a whole new world of insight and personal growth opened up through contact with other survivors. Almost immediately I became hooked on the power and resourcefulness of peer support, mutual aid among those with cancer histories.

This experience led to the creation of a local cancer support organization, Living Through Cancer (LTC). Starting with a conference attended by 135 cancer survivors and their loved ones, the organization has developed into a very special community, a network of cancer survivors and their loved ones. Now six years old, the LTC community sponsors a variety of programs including support groups, one-to-one support, a telephone helpline service, social pot-lucks, a lending library, and an educational journal. The organization, which had a total attendance of more than 850 in support groups last year, now has two full-time paid staff, as well as several staff volunteers. Scores of other volunteers participate in LTC programs.[6]

Bereavement—mourning the death of a child, spouse, or other loved one—is one of the most traumatic periods of an individual's lifetime. Because it affects people's lives psychologically, socially, and often materially and economically, it is not surprising that many self-help groups have been set up to help people cope with these losses. The national president of The Compassionate Friends, the largest self-help group for bereaved parents and siblings, has written of its origin and her experience:

In October 1975 while my husband and I were vacationing, our eight year old son Daniel was fatally injured on his way home from school. We were left to resolve our grief alone, isolated from the community, family and friends. There was no Compassionate Friends at that time. Only a few widely separated independent groups existed around the country.

Three years later some 40 of these groups gathered in Chicago to form the national organization. Another bereaved parent in my community heard about TCF and announced her desire for a local chapter. Together we united with a third bereaved parent to form the Mercer Area (NJ) Chapter. Our first meeting in November 1979 included 15 bereaved parents.

Although I thought I was simply helping other bereaved parents to avoid the isolation I had experienced, I found that my own healing was greatly enhanced by the group. TCF brought me beyond mere survival to experience life with joy and meaningfulness. In a way I had never thought possible, my present life has an excitement and fulfillment even greater than that I had known when Daniel was alive.

This astonishing fact is a direct result of my involvement with TCF. As I have gone from the local to the national organization, I have been forced to stretch my capabilities, to broaden my concepts and to grow in my commitment.

My family has changed, too. My husband and I have developed a closer, deeper relationship. Our two surviving sons and subsequent daughter have struggled through grief to a better understanding and appreciation of life. It is through watching their struggle that I have become committed to expanding TCF's role to encompass surviving siblings.

Through more than 600 autonomous chapters, TCF offers friendship and understanding to bereaved parents and siblings. The program includes meetings that provide both grief education and the opportunity for parents and siblings to share their stories. Additional contact and information is available through the national and chapter newsletters, library of books and tapes, telephone friends line and national and regional conferences. The greatest assistance, however, is gained when parents and siblings become involved in the TCF leadership. That is when they discover the special magic of TCF: that healing comes from sharing yourself with others and from working together for all bereaved parents and siblings.[7]

The death of a spouse and being widowed is a pervasive, hazardous experience in our kind of society, which lacks the social supports of extended families, neighborliness, and community concern for others that characterized the less highly technical, less mobile, and less urbanized societies of our past. Self-help groups for widows have existed since the late 1960s and are now widespread. A survey of recently widowed women cites a typical statement by a member: "Widows I have talked with felt that neither friends, family, physicians nor clergymen, for that matter were very helpful. . . . On the other hand, they found that other widows could be extremely helpful; they were the least likely to tell them to 'keep a stiff upper lip' at a time when the widows felt their lives were ended and any hope for the future gone. Other widows realized that grief . . . had to run its course before it was possible to feel better again" (Ogg, 2). There are now many widowed persons self-help groups, organized by churches and synagogues, the American Association of Retired Persons, social agencies, and other institutions.

The founder of a local chapter of THEOS, a group for younger and middle-aged widowed persons, describes some of her motivations and experiences:

THEOS was started because of a need to "reach outside myself" after the death of my husband—and to give back to others and return some of the wonderful support I had been given by many. Also, I think it was one way of making his death meaningful—the driving emotion that propels people to "TO DO SOMETHING" to get out of themselves after a traumatic experience. When done constructively, this is what compels people to establish something in the dead person's name, i.e., scholarships, memorials, etc., and to many cases, start self-help groups. This turning outward to others was one of the many things that pushed me faster toward recovery and helped identify me again as a single person.

Starting a self-help group such as THEOS for widowed people required, first, the spark of inspiration, then large doses of empathy and enthusiasm, and, finally, a willingness to work hard and the persistence to stick with it in the beginning to get the group firmly established and off the ground. Something I will always remember is some advice I heard at a workshop I attended in Pittsburgh to find out how to start a local chapter. It was, "Always remember, YOU are the expert, the professional—not the priest, rabbi, minister, social workers, psychologist, therapist, etc.—because you have experienced personally what everyone in your group is now experiencing." And probably the most important thing they experience is HOPE![8]

While there are many differences among them, as these firsthand accounts indicate, non-12-step self-help groups have been created for basically similar reasons and share many common features in their programs and activities. They all emphasize regular group meetings as an essential method for helping people emotionally and intellectually in their understanding of and attitudes toward the problem. They usually provide accurate information and sometimes organize material help, such as baby-sitting or respite care for those caring for someone. Many personal accounts show that these individuals have overcome feelings of isolation, loneliness, and having been specially victimized through fate, genetics, or one's own behavior. They provide the opportunity to learn to think differently about the problem and one's role in it, to learn from others new attitudes and coping skills, and to share one's experiences. In non-12-step groups these gains usually come from listening to and participating in often free-wheeling group discussions and interchanges. Improved self-esteem often results from being in a position to help others from personal experience, or to help the group itself by taking on some needed tasks or responsibilities.

## Differences between the Two Approaches

The most important difference between the two kinds of groups stems from the fact that 12-step groups universally have a strong ideology based on the idea that personal change can only be achieved through spiritual belief or conversion. Non-12-step groups, in contrast, are usually nonideological; may formulate some kind of ideology as they develop, but many do not. Similarly, non-12-step groups do not include a more or less prescribed meeting structure: they do not normally expect their members to pursue a phased path of personal growth and change, although they hope that change will occur.

An important difference between the types comes from the concept of powerlessness. The first step of 12-step programs—"We admitted we were powerless over [whatever addiction]—that our lives had become unmanageable"—sets the tone and becomes the groundwork for all that follows. The admission of personal powerlessness and the need for outside help of a spiritual kind, however defined, is expected of every new member. Non-12-step groups do not require members to accept such a fundamental idea in order to participate. In 12-step groups the admission of powerlessness and the need of a Higher Power's help is seen as the necessary precondition for forming new attitudes and adopting new empowering behavior. In the other kind of group a change of attitude and behavior is hoped for but has no spiritual connotations. Emphasized instead are learning and sharing coping skills through the group process, mutual support, practical information and advice, role examples, and so forth.

Some non-12-step groups are concerned that accepting the idea of powerlessness could inhibit physically ill or incapacitated people from exercising their maximum efforts in doing things for themselves, from an optimistic outlook that they can gain greater control over their own bodies and therefore over their day-to-day living. The 12-step groups disagree with this view, arguing that "powerlessness" does not imply passivity; the dispute, however, has not been resolved.

Another important difference between the two types is found in the time element—the expectation of how long members will remain in the organization. Acceptance of the 12 steps and the resultant personal program implies that enrolling in a 12-step group is an indefinite, even a lifelong, commitment. Members are expected to believe that without continuous involvement with the program they will not be able to remain free of the addiction. Many members of A.A. and similar groups have been in the organization for years—10-year "birthday" cakes are quite common, and 25-year memberships are not unheard of. Conversely, many non-12-step groups do not have such an expectation: in fact, some consider group membership temporary, assuming that whenever the crisis or problem that has brought in a new member is resolved, that member will probably leave the group. Groups for widowed or divorced persons have high rates of turnover: once the member has been helped to come to terms with the loss or change, the group may not be needed anymore, and those who can make it on their own are applauded, not stigmatized.

Though there is no known average length of membership in 12-step groups, another phenomenon has been noted: people may drop out for a period of time but often return to group meetings when they feel need of them. This in-and-out aspect also occurs in some non-12-step groups. For example, groups for chronically ill persons whose condition may flare up from time to time bring back members who feel they need help, advice, or emotional support.

Another major and significant difference between the two types of groups concerns ideas and practices about sociopolitical action and system change. One of A.A.'s 12 traditions, copied and adhered to by other 12-step groups, specifically prohibits the organization from taking any position or action on political or other outside issues. Tradition 10 reads, "A.A. has no opinion on outside issues; hence our name ought never be drawn into public controversy." The reason for the prohibition probably is to avoid a subject or activity on which members may not agree, and thus to avoid jeopardizing the unity and single goal of the organization. The prohibition is well-observed: 12-step groups take no position on public issues or legislation that might affect the problem they deal with (such as alcohol taxation). In contrast, many non-12-step groups support legislation and political candidates who would help their cause, and they engage in lobbying and demonstrations.

## Chapter 3

# Common Characteristics of Self-Help Groups

## Cognitive Restructuring

Mental-health clinicians use the term *cognitive restructuring* to describe the process of changing a client's perceptions and understanding of his or her problem and of how such understanding influences behavior. Leon Levy has analyzed how self-help groups facilitate members' new cognitive perceptions. According to Levy, self-help groups

1. [Provide] members with a rationale for their problems or distress, and for the group's way of dealing with it, thereby removing their mystification over their experiences and increasing their expectancy for change and help. . . .
2. [Provide] normative and instrumental information and advice. . . .
3. [Expand] the range of alternative perceptions of members' problems and circumstances and of actions which they might take to cope with their problems. . . .
4. [Enhance] members' discriminative abilities regarding the stimulus and event contingencies in their lives. . . .
5. Support . . . changes in attitudes toward one's self, one's own behavior, and society. . . .
6. [Reduce or eliminate] a sense of isolation or uniqueness regarding members' problems and experiences through the operation of social comparison and consensual validation. . . .

7. [Make possible] the development of an alternative or substitute culture and social structure within which members can develop new definitions of their personal identities and new norms upon which they can base their self-esteem.[1]

This quotation from the British National Council of Single Parents illustrates how group membership helps change an individual's perceptions: "Self help groups have a double value—to single parents in providing the mutual support that is so important to them, and to the children in helping them have a real social identity by understanding that there are many single parents, and the children, therefore, are not unusual in any way."[2]

Cognitive restructuring may apply to changing a member's ideas about the origin of his or her problem. For a long time mental-health professionals attributed severe mental illnesses leading to disturbed psychosocial functioning mainly to bad family relationships and environmental problems. Self-help groups arose to challenge these predominantly professional views: first the American Schizophrenic Association and then the National Alliance for the Mentally Ill (NAMI) promulgated the idea that mental illnesses such as schizophrenia and bipolar or manic-depressive conditions have an organic and biological basis. This view has been increasingly validated by research and is now widely accepted by mental-health professionals. Parents and other relatives of the mentally ill found a new perspective and changed their ideas about the problem, and their own involvement in it, when they joined a pertinent self-help group. Dr. Agnes Hatfield, a professor in education and one of the NAMI's founders, observed, "Theories of etiology and treatment . . . change as the families of mentally ill patients gain power. . . . [T]heories that stigmatize patients and families lose favor."[3]

Cancer patients and their families have also changed their perceptions about the illness through self-help-group membership. The terrors, anticipation of suffering, and feelings of doom associated with a diagnosis of cancer are often replaced for cancer patients in self-help groups by reassurance and feelings of optimism, based on both learning about recent scientific developments and sharing personal experiences with other group members.

Some of the most dramatic cognitive restructuring occurs in self-help groups of persons with physical disabilities, where the usual socially sanctioned perceptions of being "handicapped" and incapable of living normally are replaced by an optimistic sense that with some help the individual with a disability can function well, perform capably in a job, and live a relatively normal life.

Cognitive restructuring in 12-step groups is a complex, structured process and is usually expected to take a long time. Indeed, the 12-step recovery program in which new and old members are involved is designed to bring about changes in perception of the problem, as well as changes in individual behavior.

A.A.'s step 1—"We admitted we were powerless over alcohol—that our lives had become unmanageable"—is in itself a beginning of cognitive restructuring concerning the ability to handle one's problem. Similarly, step 2—"Came to believe that a Power greater than ourselves could restore us to sanity"—through step 4, which calls for making a candid, fearless self-appraisal, followed by making amends to those one has wronged, require reappraisal and a change of perceptions and beliefs (*AA*, 314). So although it is a specifically structured process and has components that differ from those in the non-12-step groups, cognitive restructuring is a major element and goal in 12-step organizations regardless of the addiction being dealt with.

## Learning Adaptive Skills

Levy's analysis speaks of providing "normative and instrumental information and advice," where *normative* means what the group has found to be useful to members. The "norm" may be as complicated as parents' expectations about the future of their handicapped child or as simple and concrete as the kind of shoes a recovering stroke patient will find easiest to put on without assistance. Phyllis Silverman and Diane Smith quote an ileostomy group member: "I learned a lot of practical things. They told me where to get the Medic-Alert bracelet and the shower-bib. They also reminded me [that] . . . it's important to eat slowly."[4]

This dissemination of information is part of most self-help-group meetings, and it is especially important for new members. Advice on where to buy services, medicines, and appliances and on shortcuts for doing so, as well as advice on which procedures are effective in applying for public aid, are topics very often discussed at group meetings. A special advantage of some groups is that they consist of a mixture of people who are at different stages of dealing with their problem. New members learn about sources of aid and assistance from those who have been through a similar period of anxiety and are able to relate their varied experiences in coping with it. My study of parents of children chronically ill with hemophilia, for example, showed that among the important skills parents learned in the group were how to care for their ill child, how to deal with sibling reactions, how to monitor their child's treatment, and how to deal with their child's school system.[5]

In addition to the kind of information gained informally from others at meetings, many groups have formal educational programs that include talks by professionals who are knowledgeable about technical aspects of the problem and research developments, and these presentations are usually followed by question-and-answer periods. Some groups also invite qualified people to teach methods of relaxation for stress reduction, pain control, and behavior change. At 12-step meetings speakers are often invited from other units of the same organization because they have a particularly inspirational message, experience, or viewpoint to convey.

Most self-help groups also publish newsletters that, in addition to organizational matters (forthcoming activities, etc.), contain articles on the particular problem—late medical discoveries, symptoms, diet, coping methods—written from the patient viewpoint. National groups bring out special brochures and even books on coping methods and strategies to further their educational aims.

## Emotional Support

Emotional support is the most sought after and widely provided category of help in self-help groups, and it is probably the one most significant to the majority of members. Seeking help from others who have the same problem is one of the major attractions to self-help groups. Margaret Yoak and Mark Chesler's study of 43 self-help groups from around the United States whose members were parents of children with cancer found that 70 percent of the groups consciously and specifically provided formalized emotional support at their meetings.[6] In a study of 80 members of nine self-help groups, Bob Knight et al. concluded that "social support is the most salient dimension of helping to the members." They state further that "the distinction between friendship and therapy, important in professional helping, . . . seems to vanish in these groups."[7]

Emotional support may take many forms and occurs in a variety of self-help-group processes. In a study of two forms of self-help groups that they referred to as "behavior control" and "stress coping," Richard

Wollert et al. developed a list of 18 "helping processes" and had members report and evaluate their occurrence at group meetings:

> The writers' "behavioral control" groups included 12-step organizations such as A.A. and Overeaters Anonymous and non-12-step groups—Take Off Pounds Sensibly (TOPS) and Parents Anonymous—where "the primary objective is some form of conduct reorganization or behavioral control." "Stress Coping" groups were differentiated as those in which members share a common stressful predicament and where the group's primary objective is to ameliorate this stress.[8]

Ten of the 18 helping processes that group members were asked to evaluate clearly express or provide emotional support. The researchers descriptions were

[1] *Positive reinforcement*: The group applauds or rewards desirable behavior.

[2] *Sharing*: Group members share everyday experiences, thoughts or feelings with other members.

[3] *Offering feedback*: Group members disclose their feelings and impressions about one another in "face-to-face" interactions.

[4] *Reassurance of competence*: Members assure one another that they are capable of handling their problems.

[5] *Justification*: Members let other members know that they were justified in feeling or acting as they did in response to some situation.

[6] *Mutual affirmation*: Members assure one another that they are valuable, worthwhile persons.

[7] *Empathy*: When a person expresses emotions in the group, other group members let that person know that they understand and share his [or her] feelings.

[8] *Normalization*: When a person describes his actions or emotions as somehow strange or abnormal, other group members assure him [or her] that his [or her] behavior is normal.

[9] *Instillation of hope*: Group members reassure other members that their problems will be worked out positively.

[10] *Catharsis*: The group facilitates the release of emotions. (Wollert et al., 37–38)

## Personal Disclosure

Personal disclosure is a feature of many self-help groups, especially 12-step groups. Members disclose to other members very personal experiences, thoughts, emotions, or fantasies that they normally would not reveal to other people. Encouragement of such personal revelations is heightened by several factors. First, the compact of confidentiality specifies that what is discussed in the group meeting is never to be repeated outside it. The 12-step groups bolster confidentiality by making strict confidentiality a "tradition," often symbolizing it by including the word *anonymous* in their names and identifying members by first name only. Many non-12-step groups follow the same precepts and procedures.

A.A.'s founders were, as I have noted, very much influenced by religious ideas, especially the Protestant Oxford Group, some of whose practices A.A. incorporated into its methodology and meetings—self-disclosure of personal failures or transgressions, making restitution to people one had wronged, and so forth. Taking personal responsibility in such ways has a long history in the Christian tradition of confession, and self-disclosure in self-help groups does have a confessional aspect. This kind of confession could not, however, be practiced in the group if people are blamed or criticized for what they reveal. *Acceptance, nonjudgmentalism, attitudes of tolerance, and continuing support,* even if the revelation seems shameful or shocking, are key features of most 12-step groups and of those non-12-step groups that emphasize emotional support and encourage sharing and disclosure.

Nonjudgmental attitudes come into play when, after making a personal revelation, the member is asked by others for additional information or explanations, but not in a challenging, confrontational, or judgmental way. Acceptance of the revelation is often shown by other members bringing out similar experiences, feelings, or thoughts. For instance, members of a group of parents of severely mentally retarded children heard a new member

> express her great feelings of disappointment about the child's appearance and mental capacity. She stated that often she hated the child, wished he'd never been born, and sometimes felt like killing him if she could get away with it. She was crying and very upset while she said these things, and looked at other members fearfully for their reactions. Two mothers in the group spontaneously hugged the speaker, saying they too had had such

thoughts. The discussion leader then asked for a show of hands as to how many in the group had shared such feelings; half the hands went up.[9]

This kind of empathetic sharing—when group members react to an expression of emotion by letting the spokesperson know they understand and share the feeling—is an important basis of emotional support wherever it is offered.

## Socialization

Comments by group members such as those quoted in Chapter 2 show how important is the groups' function of helping overcome feelings of social isolation of affected individuals and families. It is well-documented that a powerful initial reaction of sufferers is "Why did it happen to me?" This reaction is often followed by social withdrawal, based on the belief that no one else (a) has the problem, (b) can understand what it means to have the problem, or (c) can help in overcoming the problem. Such isolation, especially if the "problem" is a socially stigmatized one, is one of the burdens many problem carriers impose on themselves—and the socialization and group integration that help the individual overcome this isolation are generally not available through individual therapy with a professional.

Yoak and Chesler's study of groups of parents of children with cancer found that "social activities were on the agenda for most groups (81%) providing a setting within which people could gather informally, enjoy a sheltered time for both children and parents during which cancer was not perceived as a stigma, and engage in recreational programs, parties and picnics." Testimony about how participating in a group makes people feel less isolated is abundant. Silverman and Smith quote from an interview with parents of a mentally retarded child:

> That experience taught us about the value of groups. You know, when you have a health problem, you tend to ask yourself, "Why me?" Your friends are all "normal." We found out that others put up with more than we do. It sometimes makes you feel lucky. You find out that others deal with some of the same things you do. The more we went to the meetings, the more we liked it. We liked what the group was doing and saw that it really was patients helping other patients, all on a volunteer basis. (Silverman and Smith, 83)

Similar testimonials pervade the newsletters, pamphlets, and books published by self-help groups of all kinds. *Alcoholics Anonymous*, the A.A. Big Book, first published in 1939 (with a second edition in 1955 and a third in 1976), contains many personal stories that emphasize the group's socializing benefits.

## Taking Actions Together

Taking actions together is another potent factor in overcoming isolation. Descriptions of self-help groups often show that one of their solidifying features is that they agree on and involve at least some members in various actions, some of which I have already mentioned—activities to build membership, raise funds, and publicize the importance of the problem.

It has long been recognized that action to do something about one's problem is a very important antidote to anxiety and feelings of helplessness. New group members are often not ready to take on any actions, either within or outside the group. Until they have been helped to work through the psychological and social stresses of their own situation, they do not have the morale or energy to make possible their doing work for the organization. This holds true for both non-12-step and 12-step groups but may be particularly common in the latter. Working through and coming to some realization that personal problems can be dealt with may take some time and effort, and doing so becomes a precondition for readiness to take some action on nonpersonal issues. All the characteristic processes in self-help groups of both types support and encourage such readiness. Some group members, however, never reach such a stage. Chapter 7 discusses in detail the fact that there are group members who never take on any responsibilities for action beyond attending meetings. In general, self-help groups accept and support such inactive members and recognize that, as in many membership organizations, only a minority of members will become truly active contributors.

Once members are ready to assume some tasks, however, they find real satisfaction in collective efforts. Participants in small working subgroups get personal satisfaction, positive feedback, and the opportunity to discuss their problems informally. Being involved in a wide range of group activities helps the member develop a new perspective that transcends obsessive concerns with his or her own problem.

One level of group activities relates to helping solve the group's specific problem. As David Robinson writes, "Alcoholics Anonymous' whole program of activities can be seen as a series of opportunities for members to help each other to handle their alcoholism. From merely telling his [or her] own drinking story at a group meeting to 12th stepping and sponsoring newcomers, the A.A. member is actively helping fellow members."[10]

Those who feel they have benefitted from being in a self-help group speak of "getting involved," "making a contribution," "doing something for the group," and so forth. Most groups provide opportunities to take part in various activities—working on the group newsletter; helping to print or photocopy announcements of special events; replying to inquiries from professionals, the public, or potential members; contacting other groups or influential people in the community; and handling press releases or other publicity. There are plenty of tasks members can assume once they are ready. The important point here is that such sharing of activities and experiences is a powerful offset to isolation and provides opportunities for new friendships.

## Empowerment, Self-Reliance, and Self-Esteem

All the self-help-group processes summarized in the preceding six categories influence how members feel about themselves. It would be difficult—and in any event irrelevant—to single out which processes have the greatest effect. Quantification is almost impossible because group members differ in their psychological makeup, individual needs and reactions, ability to respond, and tempo of change and growth. Additionally, the processes and categories we have used often interact and overlap: essentially abstractions, they are useful for analyzing what goes on in groups but do not function independently. Personal and psychological change always involves multiple causes and components. We can, however, generalize that a common goal and frequent result of exposure to these socially influential factors in self-help groups is an increase in members' self-reliance and self-esteem.

Psychologists use the term *self-concept* to mean "the image or mental picture one has of one's self, a set of attitudes about one's own mental and physical capabilities. . . . One judges oneself by others' standards, and uses feedback from the overt or sensed reaction of others, as guides to immediate action and as predictors of what behaviors will be appropriate in the future."[11] Closely related is the psychological entity of self-esteem, which "can be conceptualized as a judgment an individual reaches and maintains concerning his personal worth" (104).

From these summary statements it is clear that the individual formulates his or her self-concept and self-esteem according to the appraisal of others. Much of self-help-group activity is designed, explicitly or indirectly, to influence positively its members' self-concept and self-esteem. Changing one's perception or attitude, acquiring information, learning coping skills, being emotionally supported, being listened to, using one's own experience to help others in the group, taking on group tasks successfully—all this affects the self-concept and self-esteem. Growth in the individual's self-reliance is paralleled by growth in the group's self-confidence. Members come to feel that they can solve or cope with their personal problems and that the group is an effective vehicle for solving the common problem that has brought them together.

The prominent social psychologist Albert Bandura has developed the closely related concept of "self-efficacy" through much empirical research on individual problem solving and the learning of new behavior.[12] Bandura uses self-efficacy to analyze and measure the individual's sense of his or her ability to handle *specific* tasks. Whereas self-concept and self-esteem reflect both a historical development and are stimulated by many people and events, self-efficacy arises from present experience with the task at hand. Spread over experience with many tasks and situations, self-efficacy can be a potent contributor to a positive self-concept and self-esteem. It is also a useful way of looking at many of the group processes where it is appropriate to learn a new coping skill or attitude. (I discuss further in Chapter 4 Bandura's ideas about how individuals incorporate social-learning influences in their own cognitive structures and behavior; there I analyze why and how the processes described in this chapter seem to work.)

"Empowerment" has become a very popular shorthand way to describe the purposes of many popular social movements, such as those of women, the aged, homosexuals, and various minority groups. It is clear that empowerment of members, sought consciously or not, occurs in many self-help groups, especially the successful and enduring ones. Much of what is presented in this and subsequent chapters underlines the role of self-help groups in empowering previously isolated and powerless individuals.

## Chapter 4

# What Makes Self-Help Groups Work?

The evidence from which I have drawn makes it apparent that self-help groups are doing something that their founders and members find beneficial, rewarding, and useful. Otherwise they would neither last nor continue to be created at such a steady pace. Why is this so? What occurs in self-help groups that gives individual members satisfaction and commands their loyalty and, in many cases, hard work on a voluntary basis? To answer these questions this chapter reviews some psychological and sociological analyses applicable to self-help groups and presents in detail two conceptual approaches—the application of social learning theory and of knowledge of functioning of the human immune system to self-help-group analysis—that seem to provide the most useful explanations to date and to be the most promising for further development of theory and research.

## Maslow's "Hierarchy of Needs"

After Sigmund Freud's pioneering formulations of the driving forces in human behavior, one of the broadest and most influential theories of human motivation is that of Abraham Maslow, which successfully integrates psychoanalytical insights about conscious and subconscious processes with other biological and social factors. Maslow's well-known analysis places human needs in a hierarchy or pyramid of five major categories.[1]

At the bottom of Maslow's pyramid are physiological needs such as food, water, and sleep. In times of external stress or deprivation these basic needs become the most urgent priority. Next come the human needs for security or personal safety, which can be satisfied negatively by removing or reducing personal fear or anxiety and positively by making reliable social arrangements that provide law and order and protection for the individual.

Maslow's third needs category is directly pertinent to the self-help field—the need for belongingness, affection, and social acceptance. The absence of a loving partner, a satisfying family life, or friends produces suffering and loneliness, which, as the firsthand accounts in earlier chapters show, characterize many people who join self-help groups. Maslow phrases his fourth category as the need for esteem, which includes self-esteem and the esteem of others. Both have been frequently evoked as motivations for affiliating with self-help groups.

Maslow's fifth and final category is the need for self-actualization, which he believes surfaces only when the lower needs in his hierarchy have been satisfied. To Maslow, self-actualization is the need to fulfill one's potential by becoming everything one is capable of, thus achieving a sense of peace and stability. It is clear that this ultimate need also provides some individual motivation for participating in self-help groups, especially those of the 12-step variety.

Almost all people who join and participate in self-help groups have a sense of personal suffering or unease, feel troubled and unable to cope with their problems alone, and seek aid and support from others. Their psychological and physical pain are often linked. Social withdrawal and feelings of rejection or of being victimized by fate frequently accompany suffering and pain. Participating in a group may be seen as a specific antidote that substitutes a sense of acceptance and understanding by others for suffering and isolation.

## Explaining the Effects of Groups

To answer the questions of why and how self-help groups work, it is necessary to look further at the processes that occur at meetings and through other group contacts. Are these simply the well-known phenomena found in most small groups, as analyzed by the field of group dynamics, or are there some additional features and processes specific or even unique to self-help groups?

Obviously a major factor in the effectiveness of self-help groups is the group process itself. Marshall Clinard offers a typical group-dynamics analysis of the effects on the individual group participant: "The group helps to integrate the individual, to change his conception of himself, to make him . . . the solidarity of the group behind the individual, and to combat social stigma. . . . The group processes, it is felt, replace 'I' feelings with 'We' feelings, give the individual the feeling of being in a group, and redefine certain norms of behavior."[2] These general group-dynamics principles apply to self-help groups, which support members, set expectations and norms on the ways members should behave, provide feedback to members on how well they are dealing with their common problems, help in "cognitively redefining" members' problems, and, above all, give members the feeling of peer solidarity in confronting and acting on the situation they mutually confront.

Writers on group dynamics have surprisingly ignored self-help groups in their research and theoretical discussions, however, and they have not applied their analytical principles to self-help group phenomena. In 1970 I attempted this task, reviewing small-group processes in general and identifying some that were particular to self-help groups. I identified a series of processes that can usefully be applied in the analysis of self-help-group phenomena:

1. Peer or primary group reference identification.
2. Learning through action; attitude and knowledge change through experience and action.
3. Facilitation of communication because members are peers.
4. Enhanced opportunities for socialization.
5. Breaking down of individual psychological defenses through group action, open discussion, and confrontation.
6. Emotional and social support of members by one another; reduction of social distance among them as compared with the distance traditionally maintained from agency staff or professionals. This enhances the therapeutic qualities of group participation.
7. Provision of an acceptable status system within which the member can achieve his place. Status is defined according to group goals and needs, and the individual's status within the social system of the group can be relatively clearly defined.
8. Simulation of or proximity to conditions of the outside world in the groups, as compared with the institutional setting or professional client-practitioner relationship.
9. The "helper" principle enunciated by [Frank] Riessman, which holds that in helping others, group members achieve personally therapeutic goals for themselves.[3]

Social-science theorists have put forth a considerable number and variety of psychological and sociological explanations since the time of that writing, a few of which have been tested in empirical studies of self-help groups. Miriam Stewart summarized a variety of theoretical approaches in a detailed 1990 review article:

AFFILIATION
Affiliation under stress improves performance; individuals seek out others sharing the same experience to help define and comprehend their reactions.
COPING
Constantly changing cognitive and behavioral efforts to manage specific external and/or internal demands that are appraised as taxing or exceeding the resources of the person.
DEVIANCE
EMPOWERMENT
A sense of control over one's life in personality, cognition, motivation; expresses itself at the level of ideas about self-worth, being able to make a difference.
GROUP
Mutuality, in group theory terms, means agreement. Group norm development and peer assessment are relevant to explicit sharing of goals.[4]

These concepts from psychology and sociology are useful in describing the *effects* of participating in self-help groups but not the mechanisms or processes that bring these effects about.

## Social-Learning Theories

**Role Modeling** A number of other concepts that Stewart reviews are from the writings of social-learning theorists and researchers, whose formulations seem to considerably extend and deepen those of group dynamicists and are especially important in the understanding of what happens in self-help groups. Probably the most applicable and best known of social-learning concepts is *role modeling*. According to Albert Bandura,

virtually all learning phenomena resulting from direct experience occur on a vicarious basis by observing other people's behavior and its consequences over time. The capacity to learn by observation enables people to acquire rules and integrated patterns of behavior without having to form them gradually by tedious trial and error. The constraints of time, resources and mobility impose severe limits on the types of situations and activities that can be explored directly. Through social modeling people can draw on vast sources of information, exhibited and authored by others, for expanding their knowledge and skills . . . seeing modeled behavior succeed for others increases the tendency to behave in similar ways whereas seeing behavior punished decreases like tendencies.[5]

Role modeling occurs frequently and is an important component of self-help-group processes. Encountering peers at various stages of coping with the problem or who have been longer in the group, a new member gains a variety of human models for learning new attitudes toward the problem, new stress-coping techniques, and new social skills. Such modeling has been explicitly reported in research on self-help groups for new mothers, anorexics and bulimics, child-abusing parents, stroke patients, and others. Bandura adds that the vicarious experience of learning from another person's attitudes or behavior can be both direct and personal, or of what he calls a "symbolic" nature (1985, 87). Learning from observing others in a group enables new participants to avoid time-consuming, trial-and-error behavior and to internalize rules or behavior patterns that lead to successful coping. These internalized rules may then serve as symbolic guides to action, making direct reinforcement from personal contact with the role model no longer necessary.

**Social Comparison** The role-model experience in self-help groups stimulates a subjective process of social comparison: "If he/she can do it, I can too." If the new member feels that there is similarity between the model's life history and his or her own, the model's influence may be greater. Many self-help groups include people at different stages of coping with a problem and thus offer a diversity of models, with varying characteristics, from which the individual can choose.

With such a variety of models available the new member can "place" himself or herself in comparison with others in the group. Positive self-appraisal is enhanced by comparing oneself to the "lesser attainment of others and diminished by using the accomplishments of the more talented as the relative standard of adequacy."[6] Observing successful coping by others raises the observer's belief in his or her personal ability to master similar tasks: "Modeling may rely on masterly models who perform calmly and faultlessly, or on coping models who begin fearfully but gradually overcome their difficulties by determined coping efforts."[7] Learning by self-comparison with others who have struggled with the problem is common and effective in self-help groups; it occurs in the regular ritual of giving and listening to personal testimonials at A.A. and other 12-step-group meetings, and it is also found at many meetings that do not follow the 12-step pattern.

**Self-Efficacy** Bandura has also developed the concept of self-efficacy to summarize an individual's sense of personal ability to perform tasks and cope with new and challenging situations. Self-efficacy is a narrower concept than self-esteem, as discussed by Maslow and others, but obviously forms part of it.

Self-efficacy also relates to the modeling process in self-help groups. The individual sense of self-efficacy arises from both direct experience and comparison of the self with others. According to Bandura, "In social cognitive theory, perceived self-efficacy results from diverse sources of information conveyed vicariously and through direct experience. . . . Modeling influences that convey effective coping strategies can boost the self-efficacy of individuals who have undergone many experiences confirming their inefficacy. Even the self-assured will raise their perceived self-efficacy if models teach them better ways of doing things" (1986, 412).

**Symbolic Modeling** Bandura believes that a model can be chosen and emulated even without face-to-face contact in a group. In this way, what he terms symbolic modeling "can transmit simultaneously knowledge of wide applicability to vast numbers of people" (Bandura 1986, 44). Again, very pertinent to self-help groups are the examples from tradition and group literature of persons who have coped successfully with the problem. A.A. books and similar publications of other 12-step organizations become guidance texts for members progressing through the 12 steps.

This form of modeling can also be instructional. It is a process that not only occurs spontaneously but may be consciously promoted and used. Bandura refers to such usage as "guided enactive modeling," which, in combination with spontaneous modeling, increases the potential for improving individual attitudes and behavior in a group setting. Self-help groups use "enactive" modeling in various ways: by highlighting the accomplishments of successful achievers and suggesting how they can be emulated; by quoting from inspirational literature with a "you can do it, too" message; by pointing out examples of successful problem coping;

and, as in Recovery, Inc. (a non-12-step group for mentally troubled people), by teaching members a specialized vocabulary to analyze one's reactions and behavior in troubling everyday situations.

**Collective Efficacy: Social Support** Bandura has added to the concept of personal self-efficacy that of "collective efficacy," which refers to group members' shared sense of their collective ability to master tasks (1986, 483). Bandura's social-learning writings have begun to acknowledge the importance of social support as an influence on self-perceived efficacy and individual functioning: "Mutual social support boosts the power of incentives by providing performance aids and heightening group participation through mutual social influences and mobilized peer support."

It is important to note that readiness to be influenced by others in one's social environment—to observe, learn from, and incorporate the attitudes and behavior of respected leaders, elders, and peers—results, at least in part, from socializing experiences that begin in infancy and early childhood. The infant's primal interactions with parents, especially the mother; the infant's development and testing of its sensory, cognitive, and motor capacities; the toddler's acquisition of language and of the expected norms of social behavior—all these entail give-and-take interactions obtainable only through human associations. While each individual is unique, the social imprinting of such patterns of thinking, reacting to, and learning from social stimuli is universal. Each member of a self-help group thus embodies and brings to it a socially patterned but individually distinctive capacity to respond to and be influenced by others. Individual differences of such kind have a lot to do with the important issue of who can benefit from and will remain in a self-help group and who will not find it helpful and will drop out.

## Social Learning and Immunological Competence

Other questions still need to be discussed for a more complete understanding of the learning and behavior-influencing processes that occur in self-help groups. How and why do the effects of modeling and group participation influence an individual? Social-learning theory has not been much concerned with underlying biological and physiological processes, yet recent research and theory analyzing immune-system processes give important and useful clues to explaining the therapeutic and preventive effects that arise from social support and group participation.

Public-health physicians and other epidemiologists have conducted many studies seeking to establish how sociopsychological factors like loneliness and social support affect human physiological processes or properties. A large, well-known study of social networks and health in northern California confirmed three hypotheses: (a) that there is an association between social isolation and poor health practices; (b) that isolation contributes to depression and inability to cope; and (c) that social isolation causes physiological changes that in turn increase susceptibility to disease.[8] Relatedly, research over the past 20 years has demonstrated that persons who receive adequate social supports have an improved health status and lower illness and mortality rates, compared with those who are isolated and unsupported. Immune-system processes are increasingly being shown to be the factors that explain these differences.

Researchers in the new field of psychoneuroimmunology have pinpointed specific changes in immune-system processes that correlate with social stresses, psychological moods, and social support. According to Stewart, "Psychoneuroimmunology is concerned with the complex bidirectional interactions between the central nervous system and the immune system. This interaction appears to play a part in psychosocial influences on immunologically resisted and mediated illnesses." From this vantage point, support systems have "been shown experimentally to influence susceptibility to some infections and to some aspects of the humoral and cell mediated immune response."[9] Epidemiological studies show that people exposed to recent life stresses are more vulnerable to hypertension, upper respiratory disease, allergies, cardiac death, and coronary disease.[10] Studies of widowed individuals have shown that after bereavement they experience gradual immune-system depressions and are particularly at risk for physical illness and early death, especially from heart attacks.[11]

Stewart elaborates on the pertinence of these findings to the operation of self-help groups:

> The psychoneuroimmunological empirical studies which have particular significance for self-help groups are those focusing on the physiological and immunological changes associated with bereavement, loneliness, and social isolation. Self-help groups offer compensatory social ties through counteracting feelings of loneliness and uniqueness by creating a sense of community. Self-help groups for bereavement, divorce and other social losses can enhance coping with loneliness and early intervention with high-risk groups

could prevent loneliness. . . . Research indicates that psychological stress associated with social-network loss or deficiency (e.g., divorce) can lead to adverse immunological changes and illness. . . . Pennebaker, Kiecolt-Glaser and Glaser demonstrated that writing or talking about an upsetting experience leads persons to understanding and has positive effects on blastogenic response of T-lymphocytes to two mitogens and on autonomic levels. Their findings "suggest that the disclosure of traumas is simultaneously associated with improvement in certain aspects of immune function and physical health." Self-disclosure in turn is a predominant form of communication in self-help groups.

How do the immunologic processes operate so that social support works its beneficial and preventive effects? The immune system has been described by Robert Ader as a "constantly vigilant sentinel dedicated to maintaining the integrity of the individual by discriminating between self and non-self, and mediating between host and pathogen."[12] And further, "It can create or induce an immunity so that, even if we are exposed to a particular pathogenic agent, it will not affect us. . . . [It] may elaborate or strengthen a particular defense so that our tolerance limits are greater. . . . [It] may go to work by activating particular cells or substances that devour or otherwise remove the disease-causing agent" (Pilisuk and Parks, 42).

As we have seen, research studies demonstrate that sociopsychological reactions can be linked to or provoke specific immune-system responses. Blood samples of people who score high on loneliness and stress indices have shown lower activity in their immune system fighter cells. Natural "killer-cell" activity in the blood has been found lower among students taking exams and subject to other stresses. Similar findings come from studies of psychiatric in-patients and, as already noted, of the recently widowed (Pilisuk and Parks, 42–61).

Not only the effects of sudden or continuous sociopsychological stresses on the immune system of individuals are under study, but also the specific effects of the individual's participation in groups, including the effects of verbal stimuli (i.e., words of praise and encouragement or of derogation and belittlement). Studied in this way—that is, in combination with analysis of the underlying immune-system processes—the power of social-learning mechanisms like modeling, social comparison, and reinforcement is better understood. Taken together, both sets of concepts/processes—social learning and the immune system—seem to be building blocks and supply the most adequate understanding to date of why self-help works. In contrast to earlier partial and descriptive formulations, these two approaches illuminate the interactive processes that occur in the groups and help to explain why and how individual members respond to them.

*Chapter 5*

# Case Studies of Two Successful Groups

This chapter traces the development of, first, a non-12-step group—the National Alliance for the Mentally Ill—and then a 12-step group—Adult Children of Alcoholics—both of which were created and became prominent in the late 1970s and 1980s. Each is, for the most part, representative of the form of self-help on which it is based. By looking at these two particular histories, we can discern the common elements in the motives for the groups' creation, their organizational structure, the programs they have developed, and what they mean to their members.

## The National Alliance for the Mentally Ill

**Impetus for Formation** One of the most prominent, fast-growing, multifaceted, and successful non-12-step self-help groups since the late 1970s has been the National Alliance for the Mentally Ill (NAMI), which has strongly affected its field of concern and provides an interesting model for other new groups.

Mental-health professionals have long understood and sympathized with the difficult situation of families of mentally ill persons, but this has not been the case for the public. Mid-nineteenth-century campaigns to improve conditions in state-run mental hospitals, led by such reformers as Dorothea Dix, often included spontaneous and informal actions by relatives of patients. The institutions were custodial: no effective medications were known, and psychological methods for treatment were not available until Freud's work at the end of the century. Relatives could do little apart from improving the material living conditions and staff attitudes at the state institutions.

The decades after World War II saw some significant advances in treatment, especially in the use of ataractics—tranquilizing drugs originally derived from plants and later chemically synthesized. These medications proved effective in reducing the agitation, hallucinations, and other thought-process and behavior disorders suffered by schizophrenics, who have traditionally been the largest diagnostic category in state hospitals. Drugs were later developed that aided patients with the so-called bipolar, or manic-depressive, syndrome. Sometimes these medications were combined with a form of psychological treatment, but the most prominent motive for their institutional use was to make patients more manageable, as individuals and in groups. By the late 1960s and 1970s mental-health professionals began to question the state-hospital function of merely maintaining sedated chronically ill patients in the back wards, believing that some of them could be helped to adapt to living in the community, given proper social supports. This belief became the rationale for the "deinstitutionalization" movement, which began about 1969 in California and other states and peaked in the late 1970s. In addition to its professional justification, which was humane and patient-oriented, deinstitutionalization had another aspect that appealed to planners and politicians: it could save states a good deal of money.

Mental-health professionals supported deinstitutionalization with the understanding that the state would provide various community medical and social services for patients discharged from hospitals. Unfortunately, these expanded community services were not a budgetary priority for state legislators; in the end, state hospitals discharged some 200,000 chronically ill patients to their families, who received little or no help. Expanded community aftercare for patients and their families was recommended by President Jimmy Carter's Commission on Mental Health in 1978 and by the Mental Health Systems Act passed by Congress in 1980, but the fiscal conservatism of the Reagan administration prevailed to abort this promise. It was this government failure to relieve families in the caretaking of patients discharged from institutions that led families to form local self-help organizations that coalesced in 1979 into the National Alliance for the Mentally Ill.

**The Constituent Groups**  In 1981 Dr. Agnes Hatfield, a professor in the College of Education at the University of Maryland, published the paper "Self-Help Groups for Families of the Mentally Ill," which gave the results of a study she had conducted in the preceding two years. Dr. Hatfield received 71 questionnaire replies from 130 mutual-help groups formed by relatives of mentally ill patients throughout the United States. She was interested in these groups' nature, length of existence, membership, organization, and so forth. She found that a large percentage had been recently formed: 77 percent were less than three years old, although 23 percent were formed before 1975. Most of the groups were small, with fewer than 50 members. Most members were parents or other relatives of mentally ill children or adults; in a majority of the groups relatives comprised between 90 and 100 percent of membership. Patients, professionals, and others numbered less than 5 percent of members in most groups. The primary objectives of most groups were (a) emotional support to families, (b) education of members, and (c) consumer advocacy. While there were variations in the nature and activities of the groups Hatfield reported on, they mostly had the kinds of meeting formats, programs, publications, and fund-raising activities characteristic of non-12-step groups.

Dissatisfaction with treatment of their mentally ill relatives and lack of communication with professionals prompted two families in California to organize Parents for Mental Recovery in May 1972. A group of eight former mental-hospital patients in San Antonio, Texas, in May 1974 got a Texas state charter for a group called Reclamation, Inc. In San Mateo County, California, a group called Parents of Adult Schizophrenics arose in 1974 from a meeting attended by people whose names were on a mailing list obtained from a San Francisco social agency. Ten people attended the initial meeting, but within a year the organization had 115 members. One of its first actions was a sit-in at the office of then-Governor Ronald Reagan to improve conditions in California mental hospitals. Similar family groups sprang up in other parts of California, and by 1977 seven local groups had formed in the San Francisco Bay area and held joint meetings under the name California Association of Families of Mentally Disabled. In the East and Midwest Pathways to Independence was founded in Virginia in 1975; groups in Wisconsin and New Hampshire followed suit.[1]

Since about 1976 groups have been springing up in state after state. These family organizations had no central means of communication; when they heard about similar groups they corresponded, exchanged newsletters, sometimes copied program and advocacy efforts. But while California had formed a state body by 1978, no national organization existed to bring the scattered family groups together.

This problem was discussed in November 1978 by the board of directors of a Wisconsin group, the Alliance for the Mentally Ill (AMI) of Dade County. Two members were asked to explore the possibility of convening a national conference in Madison, with participation of groups from all parts of the United States. A letter to groups nationwide drew much encouragement for going ahead with planning for a national meeting. A $5,000 grant was received under the U.S. Higher Education Act, which defrayed expenses, and all participant fees were to be kept minimal.

The conference planning group included the president and three other members of the Wisconsin AMI, three academics from the University of Wisconsin, and an official of the Wisconsin State Health and Social Services Department. The planning group's objectives included

> To foster learning about federal legislation, current research, and recent developments in the treatment of persons which chronic mental illness.
> To encourage sharing what citizens can do through mutual help/advocacy groups in improving the lives of mentally ill persons and their families.
> To create a national federation, coalition, or network of local and state mutual help/advocacy groups. (*NAMI,* 5–7)

The founding conference was held in Madison on 7–9 September 1979, and the keynote speaker was Dr. Hatfield, who had been associated with a Maryland group and was later NAMI president (1982–83). The conference was attended by 284 people representing 59 groups from 29 states and Canada. They heard presentations from the director and other officials of the National Institute of Mental Health (NIMH), mental-health professionals, family members, and former patients. All participants worked on one of five task forces: (a) purpose, (b) structure, (c) program, (d) communications, and (e) funding. At the final session a resolution to incorporate the National Alliance for the Mentally Ill was unanimously adopted. Some conferees disagreed with the chosen name, preferring that it reflect the fact that most members were parents and that schizophrenia was the most serious mental disease.

**The NAMI's Early Years** At the Wisconsin conference a geographically diverse steering committee composed of 12 members plus alternates was elected, and the committee subsequently chose officers for the first year: president, two vice-presidents, secretary, and treasurer. In "A Recollection of the Early Years" Shirley Starr, NAMI president from 1980 to 1982, wrote of the founding conference, "The weekend in Sept. 1979 that resulted in the formation of the National Alliance for the Mentally Ill was a weekend filled with 18-hour work days and the burning conviction that the 284 individuals present were part of a movement for which the right time had come and that each person was no longer alone in confronting mental illness in the family" (*NAMI*, 8).

The work of the new national organization commenced at once. Conference participants had contributed or pledged $4,000 to meet essential expenses before the NAMI could secure nonprofit status from the Treasury Department. The steering committee met in February 1980 and heard some promising reports on recognition of the NAMI by the media, mental-health professionals, the NIMH, and other organizations. A voting formula was adopted, based on membership size of the affiliates, and the NAMI was incorporated as a nonprofit corporation in Missouri with temporary offices in St. Louis, in the law firm of its first president, George Hecker.

The main discussions at the second annual NAMI conference in Chicago in September 1980 concerned the hiring of an executive director and the location of the permanent national office. The president was authorized to define the job specifications and to start a search for a suitable appointee. After considerable discussion it was decided to locate the office in Washington, D.C., rather than Chicago, because of the former's proximity to Congress and federal agencies concerned with mental health. Before the second conference NAMI leaders had spent a good deal of time in Washington, making contacts with federal officials and legislators and explaining the new organization's purposes and objectives. Contacts were made with the Mental Health Liaison Group, which was composed of all organizations that dealt with mental illness; it accepted the NAMI as a member in the summer of 1980. In 1981 a $100,000 grant was received from the MacArthur Foundation of Chicago, making possible the opening of an NAMI office in Washington and the hiring of an executive director in May of that year.

Reviewing the NAMI's early development, the second president, Shirley Starr, wrote,

> We had accomplished much in two years. We had received a significant grant from a major foundation. We had moved into larger quarters. We had expanded our staff and had increased the number of volunteers 200 percent. We were an essential member of the Mental Health Liaison Group, and we were represented on the President's Committee on Employment of the Handicapped and on the American Psychiatric Association's Committee on

the Chronically Mentally Ill. Our membership had grown from the original 284 present at Madison, Wisconsin, to over 5000.

Coincident with its numerical growth and productive contacts with federal officials, the NAMI began to get increasing media attention. *Women's Day* magazine carried a favorable story in its April 1981 issue; later that year the *New Yorker* published in four installments Susan Sheehan's moving story of a schizophrenic, later published as a Pulitzer Prize–winning book, *Is There No Place on Earth for Me?* The dramatic problems of the mentally ill and their families and the NAMI's pioneering efforts in self-help were arousing wide public interest, greater than could be achieved by purely professional efforts. By the time of its fourth annual conference in Washington, D.C., in 1982, the NAMI heard reports that the organization had around 160 affiliates with 8,000 members. Later that year the first NAMI subgroup was formed, HELP (Help Exists for Loved Ones in Prison), for NAMI members who had experienced the death of a family member because of mental illness or who had mentally ill family members serving a prison sentence.

**Rapid Growth and Influence** As local affiliates of the NAMI were increasingly engaged in advocacy for services, it was recognized that the appropriate action targets were their own legislatures. The new Reagan administration was curtailing social programs as fast as possible; the national NAMI office was very active in efforts to save the Community Support Program of the NIMH, to resist Social Security reviews and cuts for disabled persons, and to increase research funding.

More state-level NAMI affiliates were organized in 1982–83: joining the California and Wisconsin state organizations were those of Colorado, Ohio, Massachusetts, New York, and Maryland. At an April 1983 board of directors meeting it was reported that the NAMI had 199 affiliated groups in 44 states; by the fifth annual conference in 1983 this figure had grown to 230 affiliates in 48 states. Again, media attention continued to multiply. The prominent psychiatrist E. Fuller Torrey lauded the NAMI on the "Donahue" television show and announced he was turning over to the NAMI all royalties from a recent book, *Surviving Schizophrenia: A Family Manual*.

The 1983 conference created a second subgroup, Siblings, for those with a mentally ill brother or sister. An Ethnic Minority Concerns Committee was also added to promote NAMI activities among ethnic minority families. In the fall of 1983 the NAMI was able to join the Combined

Federal Campaign, similar to the United Way, for federal government employees. This, in conjunction with the royalties from Dr. Torrey's book and grants from private foundations, helped to stabilize the NAMI's financial situation.

The 1983 annual conference also called for the NAMI to establish a research foundation, with both a scientific and a lay governing board. After exploration of this idea—and many discussions with government officials and private organizations concerned with mental illness—the NAMI created the National Alliance for Research on Schizophrenia and Depression in June of 1985. The foundation's bylaws required that a majority of board members be family members of the mentally ill or patients themselves. Twenty-two prominent psychiatrists were enlisted to serve on the scientific council. The main focus of research was to be serious mental illness, with emphasis on organic factors.

By October 1985 the 500th NAMI affiliate was enrolled (*NAMI*, 10).

**How the NAMI Compares with Other Non-12-Step Groups** In the 1980s the NAMI was transformed from a scattered handful of small family groups to an influential national organization with nearly 1,000 affiliates (by 1988), a varied program of activities coordinated by a national office with a sizable staff, and an annual budget of more than $1 million. In addition, some of its 20 statewide organizations have independent offices and paid staffs. The NAMI's steady, rapid, and generally harmonious growth is one of the impressive success stories among non-12-step self-help groups and has lessons that might apply to other new non-12-step groups.

Three factors seem particularly contributory to the NAMI's success: (a) the nature and extent of the need it sought to meet; (b) its combination of functions, to include both emotional support and education to family members and advocacy or social action, especially directed at federal and state legislators and officials; and (c) the quality of its leadership.

I have reviewed the first factor at length earlier in this chapter. Some 200,000 persons were discharged from state mental hospitals to the community, usually to their nuclear families, during the deinstitutionalization wave of the 1970s. Although there were promises of legislation to secure supportive community aftercare programs for these former patients and their families, the promises were not kept. The patients and their families were largely left to their own devices in adapting to community living and each other. Spontaneous self-help groups of families and patients emerged in various locations; both the numbers and the serious nature of the problems made consideration of a national organization inevitable.

The second factor was the concurrent attention given to the emotional and interpersonal issues affecting patients and families *and* to social action to influence legislators to add or increase budgets for improved service and research. From their beginnings, most of the constituent local groups recognized the importance of political action and engaged in lobbying, demonstrations, and other pressure tactics to make the public aware of their needs and to implement remedial legislation. The NAMI's office was established in Washington, D.C., specifically to have access to federal functionaries and members of Congress. Officials of the key federal agency dealing with mental illness—the National Institute of Mental Health—were extensively lobbied by the NAMI in its early years, and these efforts paid off in the acceptance and support of the organization and its purposes by legislation-affecting federal officials.

The third factor was the combination of exceptionally able, dedicated, and energetic leaders and the genuinely democratic and participatory structures they instituted. All of the leaders had the experience of a mentally ill family member. Many of them were middle-class business or professional people, self-confident and articulate in public presentations and knowledgeable of how to develop contacts with influential policy-makers and other mental-health organizations.

The organization's early-established constitution, bylaws, election procedures, and national/local relationships assured true representation in governance. The fact that national conferences were held annually, with election of the national board of directors, which in turn elected the officers, contributed to the NAMI's democratic style and helped to avoid or minimize the schisms and conflicts that have frequently impaired other non-12-step groups.

In 1991 Dr. Hatfield summed up the NAMI's development and its continuing problems:

> In many ways NAMI has been a product of its time. Deinstitutionalization was moving at a rapid pace at the time of its formation, communities were unprepared to provide services, and families bore the major burden of care. Several decades had passed since the formation of the self-organized parents' groups reported by Katz for NAMI to profit from some of their experiences. The NAMI movement developed a strong sense of self reliance because they did not assume an unquestioned wisdom on the part of professionals and they recognized conflict of interest with them. Finally

biological psychiatry had progressed to a point where it was possible to clarify and delimit the focus of the organization to "mental illness."[2]

Despite a very favorable beginning, continuing growth has begun to threaten the NAMI's grass-roots character. Members no longer know each other personally. This is especially difficult for the group's founders, who were intimates of each other and operated on a basis of trust. Local members have yet to learn politically effective ways of expressing their will to the national body.

A crucial issue that the NAMI needs to resolve is how much of a role mental-health professionals should play in the organization—an issue on which members differ widely. Some feel that professionals could easily coopt the movement; others worry about a continuing hostility toward professionals and feel that lay members need to work closely with them if these members are to benefit from their affiliation with the NAMI. Most agree that the problem is quite complex. Professionals are now involved in the organization in many ways, both locally and nationally, and two NAMI networks, the Curriculum and Training Network and the Legal Alliance, consist mostly of professionals. The pivotal question for the NAMI is to what extent it can be a large, powerful organization and still retain the innovativeness and flexibility of a young movement.

## Adult Children of Alcoholics

**The Concept of Co-Dependency**  A number of new 12-step organizations have been formed that help people deal with the cluster of problems that are now widely known as "co-dependency." *Co-dependency* refers to a situation in which a family member (or significant other) neglects personal needs because of extreme preoccupation with the needs of a person with a chemical or psychological addiction, such as alcoholism, compulsive gambling, and overeating. In a way the co-dependent has become addicted to the person with the alcohol, drug, or other compulsion. Usually such addiction to meeting the needs of another has a long history, originating in childhood in a disturbed family setting, and the situation is usually kept secret or covered up for a long time. According to psychiatrist Timmen Cermak and his colleagues, "Lay support groups probably originated the term [co-dependency] . . . [and] many co-dependent persons come to the physician self diagnosed."[3] Cermak has proposed some formal diagnostic criteria for co-dependency:

Assumption of responsibility for meeting others' needs to the exclusion of acknowledging one's own needs;

Anxiety and boundary distortions in situations of intimacy and separation;

Enmeshment in relationships with personality-disordered, drug-dependent, and impulse-disordered individuals;

Exhibition of any three or more of the following behaviors: constriction of emotions with or without concomitant dramatic outbursts: depression; hypervigilance; compulsions; anxiety; excessive reliance on denial, substance abuse, recurrent physical or sexual abuse; stress-related medical illness; or a primary relationship with an active substance abuser that lasts for at least two years without the individual seeking outside support.[4]

Co-dependency reflecting such behaviors has in the last few years become one of the most publicized and at the same time most controversial motivations for creating and joining self-help groups of the 12-step variety. Recent attacks on self-help organizations in professional publications and the media have questioned the value of the co-dependency concept and the efficacy of self-help groups in overcoming the problems it targets. Examples of such criticism are the March 1992 *American Demographics* article "Selling Self-Help" and Wendy Kaminer's 1992 book, *I'm Dysfunctional, You're Dysfunctional: The Recovery Movement and Other Self-Help Fashions.*

Prominent among proponents of co-dependency as a previously unrecognized but important form of personal addiction has been Adult Children of Alcoholics (ACA), a widely influential self-help group that began to organize in the early 1970s. According to Cermak, "Chemical-dependence specialists have more experience with the alcoholic co-dependent. . . . But they now recognize that ACA's diagnostic and therapeutic material applies to all co-dependents—to everyone in a family that is dysfunctional from whatever cause, not necessarily alcoholism" (1989, 134).

**History** After A.A. was formed in 1935, the devastating effects of alcoholism on family members became more and more recognized, and A.A. group meetings for family members began to be regularly held. They functioned widely but unofficially as a part of the A.A. program until 1951, when Al-Anon Family Groups was officially established as a separate organization under the leadership of the wife of one of the two A.A. founders.

The first mention of "children of alcoholics" was made in an Al-Anon presentation at A.A.'s Twentieth Anniversary Conference, "AA Comes of

Age," in 1955. Two years later Alateen—a support group for teenage children of alcoholics—was formed at a meeting in California. Apparently some participants grew dissatisfied with the Al-Anon and Alateen programs, finding that they were not being specifically assisted with their problems of self-abnegation and co-dependency. A 1970 meeting in New York City advertised as "Hope for Adult Children of Alcoholics" led to the creation of the first Adult Children of Alcoholics group that met outside of Al-Anon. Other meetings followed in New York over the next few years; the dimensions of the special co-dependency problems of "adult children" began to be widely discussed and chronicled by ACA initiators.[5]

In 1980 materials from the New York meetings arrived in Houston and Los Angeles, where weekly ACA meetings began to be held. The New York materials about the problems faced by adult children of alcoholics—colloquially dubbed the "laundry list"—was reworked into a more formal statement called "The Problem," which began to be used at ACA meetings organized elsewhere in California and in Portland, Seattle, and Phoenix. In 1981 a national directory listing 11 ACA groups was published. The spread of the concept and the organization was accomplished largely through the personal efforts of Los Angeles members, who conveyed meeting formats, materials, and experience to new locations.

An ACA therapy group was started in Los Angeles in 1981. Members began to publish articles about ACA, and two books appeared in 1982—*Adult Children of Alcoholics*, by Janet G. Woititz, a psychologist who had organized the therapy group, and *Co-Alcoholic, Para-Alcoholic: Who's Who and What's the Difference*, by lay member Jael Greenleaf—both of which provided important sources of discussion at ACA meetings and helped to publicize the program and recruit new members. As membership and the number of groups grew, need was felt for a coordinating body to establish and unify organizational purposes, principles, and policies. In September 1981 the first meeting of a body that came to be called the Central Service Board was held in southern California.

In 1983 the Committee on Identity, Purpose, and Relationships was established by the Central Service Board to further clarify and unify ACA's purposes, organizational structures, and relationships of its various units. The committee prepared and circulated a questionnaire, dealing primarily with ACA's identity and autonomy. At the first national ACA Business Conference in southern California in 1984, 50 ACA units were represented. The conference voted to establish ACA as an autonomous 12-step organization, separate from Al-Anon. In August 1985 papers to incorporate ACA as a not-for-profit, tax-exempt entity were filed with both the state of California and federal government. Also at this time ACA's bimonthly newsletter, *Comline*, began publication, and central phone lines and an office in a member's Los Angeles home were established. ACA contact groups and communications with independent or Al-Anon-affiliated units quickly expanded. The Central Service Board communicated with groups in 29 states and nine other countries during 1985.

At the second ACA Business Conference in 1986 the Identity, Purpose, and Relationships Committee presented the report "Finding Wholeness through Separation: The Paradox of Independence," which ended with a "Solution" that the conference adopted as the "official suggested version of ACA." The Central Service Board's functions were expanded at the 1986 conference to include those of a World Service Office for an interim one-year period. This interim arrangement was continued for another year at the fourth ACA Business Conference in 1987, but at the fifth Business Conference in 1989 the World Service Office became the Interim World Service Organization.

By January 1988 ACA had more than 1,000 independent units functioning in 43 states, five Canadian provinces, and five other countries. By April of 1990, 1,500 independent meeting groups were registered in the United States and some 200 in 10 other countries (ACA Interview, 1990).

**How ACA Compares with Other 12-Step Groups** ACA both resembles and differs from other 12-step organizations. Groups created to deal with nonchemical or psychological addictions—for instance, Gamblers Anonymous and Overeaters Anonymous—sought and received permission to borrow A.A. principles and methods and to apply the latter for the first time to the problems they were concerned with. But in the case of ACA there had been a longtime concern with the effects of an alcoholic on family members, which, as I have noted, resulted in the formation of Al-Anon in 1951 and of Alateen in 1957.

Like other newly formed 12-step groups, ACA started small and in a single location but addressed a widespread problem and had a large potential membership. Differing from other new 12-step groups because of their original affiliations with offshoots of A.A., ACA founders also had to deal with issues related to identity, autonomy, and their relationships with A.A. and other alcoholism-related organizations. While ACA grew markedly throughout the 1980s, the issues of definition and identity took up a considerable amount of its leaders' time and energy; approaches to these issues were constantly being formulated, revised, or discarded. Additionally, ACA leaders in the United States devoted much time and attention to establishing contacts and seeking mechanisms for cooperation and coordination with ACA groups in other countries, which often had different meeting formats, terminologies, and methodologies.

**Differences from A.A. Philosophy and Methods** As I have noted, ACA originated among persons who had participated in A.A. offshoot organizations, and its founders adhered to the principles and methodology embodied in A.A.'s 12 steps and 12 traditions. But the dissatisfactions that spurred ACA's initial conception and its subsequent move toward independence through an intensive process of discussion of shared experience led to a philosophy and operating principles that diverged markedly from those of its parent organizations.

ACA held the conviction that psychoanalytic approaches to recovery from alcohol or other chemical addictions were generally unsuccessful—a tenet in A.A.'s founding. ACA's founders believed that A.A.'s philosophy and programs contained some useful elements, especially relating to sociopsychological explanations for addictive behavior. But when it came to *changing* the behavior of co-dependent adult children, A.A.'s methods were not thought to be effective. Two reasons for this emerged from lengthy discussions among ACA members in the 1970s and early 1980s. The first reason was that A.A. was geared to achieving and maintaining abstinence in the problem drinker: resolution of the drinker's psychological conflicts was not seen as a necessary condition for abstinence. ACA leaders believed that identifying the symptoms of both addiction and dysfunctional behavior would not necessarily lead to or maintain an addiction-free state. Furthermore, it was noted that a number of addicted individuals resisted A.A. membership or dropped out early because they found it impossible to remain abstinent despite the program.

The second reason was that ACA leaders began to question A.A.'s concentration on the "here and now," on adhering to the approved A.A. program without necessarily delving into the past to locate causes for the addictive behavior. ACA leaders believed that achieving abstinence was not feasible for a person with serious mental and emotional problems that were not dealt with as such. According to Rhonda Elwell, "Often members of the [A.A.] program limit their recovery to the issue of chemical dependency, by 'Staying in the moment.' But, after a period of time, many members become more interested in their psychopathology and begin to resent the obedience and powerful dependency upon the groups."[6]

While "here-and-now" approaches to recovery clearly pervade A.A., ACA has developed a counter-emphasis on reviewing childhood experiences. At times the focus might still be on the here and now, but instead of dealing mainly with sobriety issues in everyday life, as summed up in the A.A. slogan "one day at a time," ACA has become concerned that members discern patterns in their childhood experiences and try to understand how these experiences affect their feelings as adults. Patterns of such disruptive feelings are analyzed at ACA meetings as arising from unpredictable and chaotic family environments, inconsistent parental nurturing, and unresponsiveness to the communication and interaction needs of the alcoholics' children. Inconsistent handling is seen as a key element, with children not knowing whether the parent will meet their emotional and physical needs at any given time.

As secrecy and denial are used to conceal the alcoholic parent's behavior, ACA believes that the child often feels pressure to join in the denial and concealment. Denial, fear, and shame thus help isolate the family members. Directly affected by the behavior of the alcoholic parent, the child experiences fear, anger, helplessness, and depression, which can persist through adult life. Feelings of powerlessness prompt coping strategies inimical to the child's own interests, and this self-damaging behavior can become habitual.

The behavioral patterns of adult children of alcoholics are thus seen to result from disrupted or negative childhood developmental processes. The "adult child" lacks the experience of a basic, trusting symbiotic relationship with the afflicted parent and becomes incapable of healthy interpersonal relationships. In fact, if the mother is an alcoholic the physically and emotionally dependent child may especially experience lack of appropriate care. If the father is an alcoholic the "co-dependent" mother may neglect the child in her preoccupation with the alcoholic husband. Natural developmental stages and tasks of childhood are thus distorted or blocked, and the child remains focused on the parents rather than on developing a sense of self.

Among other developmental deprivations of the adult child are learning to interact comfortably with peers and to acquire social skills and satisfactions, so that these adults often feel lonely and isolated. Other common characteristics as analyzed by ACA include low self-confidence; fear of abandonment, separation, and intimacy; unassertiveness; the inability to set limits; and poor communication skills.

**"The Problem" and "The Solution"** Considerably detailed descriptions of these psychological characteristics and behavior of the adult child can be found in ACA publications and in several books on ACA problems.

"The Problem" and "The Solution," ACA's official statements to guide new members and newly founded ACA units, resulted from lengthy discussion and reflect numerous revisions of earlier formulations. "The Problem" replaced the so-called laundry list of 14 psychological characteristics. Here it is in its entirety:

> Many of us found that we had several characteristics in common as a result of being brought up in an alcoholic or otherwise dysfunctional household.
>
> We had come to feel isolated, uneasy with other people, especially authority figures. To protect ourselves we became people pleasers, even though we lost our own identities in the process. All the same, we would mistake any personal criticism as a threat.
>
> We either became alcoholics ourselves or married them or both. Failing that, we found another compulsive personality, such as a workaholic, to fulfill our need for abandonment.
>
> We lived from the standpoint of victims. Having an overdeveloped sense of responsibility, we preferred to be concerned with others rather than ourselves. We somehow got guilt feelings when we stood up for ourselves rather than giving in to others. Thus, we became reactors rather than actors, letting others take the initiative.
>
> We became dependent personalities—terrified of abandonment—willing to do almost anything to hold to a relationship in order not to be abandoned emotionally. Yet we kept choosing insecure relationships because they matched our childhood relationship with our parents.
>
> These symptoms of the family disease of alcoholism made us "co-victims"—those who take on the characteristics of the disease without necessarily ever taking a drink. We learned to stuff our feelings down as children and kept them buried as adults. As a result of this conditioning, we confused love with pity, tending to love those we could rescue. Even more self-defeating, we became addicted to excitement in all our affairs, preferring constant upset to workable relationships.
>
> This is a description, not an indictment.

And here is "The Solution":

> The Solution: to become your own loving parent. As ACA becomes a safe place for you, you will find the freedom to express all the hurts and fears you have kept inside and to free yourself from the shame and blame that are carryovers from the past. You will become an adult who is imprisoned no longer by childhood reactions. You will recover the child within you, learning to accept and love yourself.

The healing begins when we risk moving out of isolation. Feelings and buried memories will return. By gradually releasing the burden of unexpressed grief, we slowly move out of the past. We learn to reparent ourselves with gentleness, humor, love and respect.

This process allows us to see our biological parents as the instruments of our existence. Our actual parent is a Higher Power some of us choose to call God. Although we had alcoholic parents, our Higher Power gave us the 12 Steps of Recovery.

This is the action and work that heals us: we use the steps; we use the meetings, we use the telephone. We share our experience, strength and hope with each other. We learn to restructure our thinking one day at a time. When we release our parents from responsibility for our actions today, we become free to make healthy decisions as actors, not reactors. We progress from hurting to healing to helping. We awaken to a sense of wholeness we never knew was possible.

By attending these meetings on a regular basis, you will come to see parental alcoholism for what it is: a disease that infected you as a child and continues to affect you as an adult. You will learn to keep the focus on yourself in the here and now. You will take responsibility for your own life and supply your own parenting.

You will not do this alone. Look around you and you will see others who know how you feel. We will love and encourage you no matter what. We ask you to accept us just as we accept you.

This is a spiritual program based on action coming from love. We are sure that as the love grows inside you, you will see beautiful changes in all your relationships, especially with God, yourself and your parents.[7]

**Growth** Among the newer 12-step groups, ACA has not been especially notable for its membership growth. It has grown steadily but not as spectacularly as such other new 12-step groups as Cocaine Anonymous, Incest Survivors, and Sex Addicts. It has nevertheless had a very important role in deepening people's understanding of co-dependency and its treatment. It has helped to make the public and health-care professionals, including physicians, aware that growing up in a disturbed family environment leaves psychological and behavioral wounds that will not heal on their own.

Although ACA founders probably originated the concept and term *co-dependency,* others picked up their ideas quickly. Co-Dependents Anonymous (CDA), an unrelated 12-step organization, was founded in 1981; this controversial, highly publicized group has probably attracted a substantial number of potential ACA members. Despite the usual 12-step principles of confidentiality, CDA representatives are much featured in media events, and the organization has probably become as well known as ACA.

## Conclusion

These case studies illustrate the spontaneous creation of self-help organizations by a few lay people with a common personal problem that they believed also affected others. For NAMI members, the problem was primarily created by the massive discharge of their grown children from state mental hospitals in the late 1960s and early 1970s. Groups of parents came together in various regions of the country for both personal help and social-policy changes; soon they created a national organization to deal especially with federal agencies and officials. They enlisted the aid of legislators and mental-health professionals to advance their aims, and—both because of the large numbers of affected families throughout the United States and effective leadership—the NAMI quickly became a well-functioning self-help organization with a strong national office and a large array of state, regional, and local units.

ACA's origin was different: it illustrates the not uncommon event that a group with particular interests and needs finds it is not getting enough attention under an umbrella-type structure. ACA members struggled for more special consideration within the Al-Anon and Alateen suborganizations of A.A. and concluded that only an autonomous organization would meet their needs. Although they retained some 12-step principles and methods, they evolved a distinctive theory and methodology that attracted people who felt damaged from growing up in households with alcoholic parents. Unlike the NAMI, ACA did not pursue mainly organizational and social goals but concentrated on personal issues. Its growth, while continuous, has been far more limited than the NAMI's.

*Chapter 6*

# Leadership, Growth Patterns, and the Role of Ideology

## Leadership-Followership

The founders of a new organization frequently do not remain in leadership positions for very long. The ability to attract attention through new ideas, effective public speaking, and media presentations does not necessarily coexist with organizational skills and the patience required for such mundane tasks as making arrangements for and conducting meetings, approaching potential members, answering inquiries, and raising and handling money. As we have seen, the majority of self-help groups started from the initiatives of a handful of people—even, as in the case of A.A., as few as two—who were anxious to do something about their common problem. They believe that there is a larger pool of people who are concerned about the problem, and they usually organize a meeting to attract others, publicizing it through personal contacts and advertising.

In my 1961 study of the development of the non-12-step groups formed by parents of handicapped children, I distinguished five stages in their growth: stage 1, *origin*; stage 2, *division of labor*; stage 3, *emergence of leadership*; stage 4, *paid staff employed* (clerical-administrative); and stage 5, *professionalization* (professionals employed for technical services clinical, public relations, fund-raising, etc., but at the behest of volunteers). I described the *origin* stage as follows:

Two or more couples whose association arose primarily through having a common interest and problem in their handicapped child, took the initiative of coming together for informal discussion as to what might be done to help themselves with their problems. After a few meetings among themselves, and perhaps with a small circle of acquaintances, an attempt was made to reach the known-to-exist wider potential membership, by having a public meeting publicized through advertising and newspaper stories. The first meeting sets off a wave of enthusiasm. The image of an action organization that helps focus public attention on their problems is created and projected . . . .

Whoever may have called together the first meetings of parents (and in the four groups in this study, only two of the originators of the first meetings went on to become significant leaders) each group at an early stage presents the opportunity for a strong leadership to emerge, usually in the person of a single individual, or in a small group of close associates.[1]

All the tasks of leadership may not be equally well accomplished by a group's founders/initiators. These are often what sociologists call "charismatic" leaders—they are articulate, well-informed, and persuasive about the problem and influence others because of their commitment and energy. In the early days of a non-12-step group, these qualities also make the leaders effective in outside contacts, in representing the group in public. Charismatic leaders may also be influential through giving advice to members about their personal problems. From activities of these kinds, the founders may for a time be the major way in which the group is identi-fied and publicly known—their names become synonymous with it. This does not usually apply in 12-step groups, however, because of their com-mitment to and tradition of preserving anonymity for all participants, including the leaders. Bill Wilson, one of A.A.'s two co-founders, wrote, "Moved by the spirit of anonymity, we try to give up our natural desires for personal distinction as A.A. members both among fellow alcoholics and before the general public. As we lay aside these very human aspira-tions . . . each of us takes part in the wearing of a protective mantle that covers our whole society and under which we may grow and work in unity."[2]

The leadership qualities needed in the early stages of self-help groups are similar to those in other informal organizations. In addition to personal articulateness and charisma, abilities to diagnose problems realistically, to reconcile or compromise conflicting viewpoints and proposals, and to take and guide the group in taking a definite stand are all needed. As the quote from Bill Wilson shows, 12-step groups mostly do not personalize or define their leadership in such ways. They are concerned to both rotate leaders and preserve member anonymity. Traditions 9 and 11 of A.A.'s 12 traditions concern leadership, organization, and anonymity:

9. Each A.A. group needs the least possible organization. Rotating leadership is the best. The small group may elect its secretary, the large groups its rotating committee, and the groups of a large metropolitan area their central or intergroup committee, which often employs a full-time secretary. The trustees of the General Service Board are, in effect, our A.A. General Service Committee. They are the custodians of our A.A. Tradition and the receivers of voluntary A.A. contributions by which we maintain our A.A. General Service Office at New York. They are authorized by the groups to handle our over-all public relations and they guarantee the integrity of our principal newspaper, the A.A. Grapevine. All such representatives are to be guided in the spirit of service, for true leaders in A.A. are but trusted and experienced servants of the whole. They derive no real authority from their titles; they do not govern. Universal respect is the key to their usefulness.

11. Our relations with the general public should be characterized by personal anonymity. We think A.A. ought to avoid sensational advertising. Our names and pictures as A.A. members ought not be broadcast, filmed, or publicly printed. Our public relations should be guided by the principle of attraction rather than promotion. There is never need to praise ourselves. We feel it better to let our friends recommend us.[3]

Leadership problems in non-12-step groups may often be more evident—for example, the acknowledged leader may have little interest in or respect for members' opinions. He or she may enjoy the prestige of leadership and relish the praise for the organization's growth but be unready to listen to and act on people's opinions and to acknowledge and help to correct personal weaknesses or leadership deficiencies. In short, the leader may be or become an autocrat and thus create difficulties and alienate members. Although there are no empirical studies on leadership discord among self-help groups, anecdotal evidence exists. Consider this example:

Members of a two-year-old self-help group of manic-depressive syndrome sufferers in a large city decided that they could no longer tolerate the dictatorial attitudes and actions of the group's charismatic founder. She ran all the group's meetings, wrote and edited its newsletter, decided on all outside invited speakers, and in meetings sharply put down any dissenting opinions. Members unsuccessfully tried to convince her to be more accepting of others and to run meetings more democratically. When she did not change, about 25 persons left the group and formed another one with similar aims but with a different name. The original leader was left with only a handful of members; she tried to build up this group again, but word of her behavior had got around, and after a few months she dissolved the original group and moved to another city.

Dissatisfaction with the climate and leadership in a local chapter or unit has occurred in 12-step groups as well, leading to dissension and the formation of a new group with the same philosophy and methods but more acceptable leadership. A southern California unit of Cocaine Anonymous has experienced such breakaway initiatives.

Such discord illustrates the question of how actively a non-12-step group's "ordinary" members—those who join to solve their personal problems and may not necessarily be willing to take on leadership responsibilities—should participate. As noted, an important defining characteristic of self-help groups is that they are "owned" by their members, who theoretically enjoy equal status with their group peers by reason of sharing the common problem. A democratic system of operation should be basic to the self-help-group structure from its earliest days. When this kind of system is absent and seems unattainable, even passive group members—"followers" who are not as committed and do not feel they know as much as the leaders/founders—may become motivated to work for change. People have differing motives for joining a group; their abilities, the time and resources they contribute to it, and their expectations of it will vary. It may take time for dissatisfactions with the actions or style of a founder to emerge, but the self-help-group structure itself gives some guarantees that democratic processes will occur.

## Development Patterns

**Non-12-Step Groups** After my earlier-mentioned five-stage "natural history" of non-12-step self-help groups was published, variant types of development emerged, necessitating that I make some revisions. For one thing, numerous self-help groups formed in the late 1960s and early 1970s specifically opposed the idea of a paid staff and thus did not pass through the model's last three stages. Organizations of this kind include a form particularly associated with the women's movement's consciousness-raising groups; some social protest groups, such as the Network against Psychiatric Assault; and groups for the widowed.

Here is how I have revised my 1961 schema:

Stage 1, *Origin*: All participants are volunteers, with little division of labor—"everyone does everything." Founder-leaders do the most and enlist others through their personal example.

Stage 2, *Division of Labor*: All activities are carried out by volunteers, but some roles get differentiated according to the availability, interest, and capacities of members who have been drawn in during or after stage 1.

Stage 3, *Emergence of Leadership*: Questioning and possible rotation of initial leadership occurs. Leadership functions and method of selection may be spelled out in a constitution or bylaws, which also differentiates and structures standing committees to carry out specific tasks.

Stage 4, *Paid Staff Employed*: The first paid staff are usually clerical workers or managers, needed to handle growing demands. Volunteers continue many functions; all decisions about program and policies are made by leaders and members.

Stage 5, *Professionalization*: Professionals or semi-professionals are employed for various technical services (i.e., clinical work, fund-raising, public relations, and accounting/bookkeeping). Theoretically, they operate under direction of volunteers—the officers, board of directors, and so forth—but because staff members address day-to-day situations, they take on responsibility for urgent decisions.

Stage 6, *Bureaucratization*: Professionals openly have a major, sometimes dominant, voice in decision-making. All the major activities are professionalized. Frequently the organizations becomes national, followed by the development of branch or regional offices. Original self-help impulses and participation of volunteers in decision-making may be diluted or dissipated.

In revising my original model, I found a decision-tree concept appropriate: that is, at different points in their history, groups face a choice that will determine their later development—whether to hire any staff at all, whether to hire a professional staff, whether to affiliate with a national organization, and so forth. Each such decision has to be made because the organization has reached a turning point in its growth—it will either get bigger and more efficient through hiring staff, or it will remain smaller and more intimate; it can affiliate with a national organization that will supply it with all kinds of literature, contacts, and other resources but may have some uncomfortable requirements and restrictions for groups that join it. The decision not to affiliate but to remain local usually means that the group prefers independence and self-reliance to growth and prestige.

Thus all groups have a stage 1, which is usually spontaneous, sometimes stimulated from the outside, through either (a) a conscious organizational effort by a previously existing group (national, regional, or local) or, less frequently, (b) an individual professional, social service, or medical institution or agency.

Similarly, all groups pass through stage 2, but not all develop more formal organizational aspects, such as a written constitution, election of leaders, and the division of labor or functions. Some groups, as usually is the case with personal-growth groups, decide on no fixed pattern of leadership (stage 3) or distribution of tasks and thus remain in stage 2. A group may decide that it wishes to remain a collectivity of volunteers, even though it has entered the stage of formal organization: the notion of employing a paid staff is rejected, and stages 4 and 5 are therefore not entered.

Many groups reach a size and scope of activities so great that they cannot be carried on by volunteers. They first hire paid staff members (stage 4), but the latter are not professionals in the sense of specially trained and credentialed persons. Much of the work of groups at this stage is still carried out by volunteers, including public-relations, accounting/book-keeping, and fund-raising activities. The decision to hire any kind of staff is often critical, provoking disagreement and even schisms, because to some members a paid staff may be incompatible with the goals of self-reliance and volunteerism.

Once any paid staff has been employed, stage 5 seems to depend on the program elements the group chooses—that is, what it wants to do—as well as on its decisions regarding scale, expansion, possible affiliation with a national organization, and so forth. The reader will note that I have added a stage 6, *bureaucratization*, which is timely in view of the expansion and growth of some non-12-step self-help groups, particularly in the health field, which become national entities.

**12-Step Groups**  I have already noted that leadership roles are quite differently conceived and handled in 12-step groups. They generally follow the A.A. principles of leadership rotation and public anonymity, as stated in A.A.'s 12 traditions. These principles reduce the possibility of personal conflicts or the chance of ambitious, autocratic, or self-serving individuals using the organization in ways that will antagonize and alienate members.

This is not to deny that in 12-step groups, as in any human organization, disagreements, conflicts, and power struggles may occur. But the guiding principles and structures of A.A.-modeled groups tend to minimize such developments and provide acceptable ways of dealing with them when they arise. Based on observations of 500 meetings of 36 different A.A. groups in California, Hawaii, and Africa, Hazle Johnson analyzed the occurrence of conflicts and schisms: "Internal adjustments (both among individuals as they are socialized or resocialized or in the way in which the group is ruled), turnover of personnel, and the formation of new groups is a constant and ongoing process in A.A. . . . A.A. is so structured that there is considerable room for change . . . and it is easy to start a new cell. Resources required are simply people and a place to meet (plus some knowledge of how a meeting is conducted)."[4]

Conflicts, dissensions, and breakaways in A.A. and other 12-step groups probably arise from the same factors that cause them in other self-help groups. These are primarily competition for various resources—power, prestige, control of assets, public recognition. In A.A. and 12-step groups generally the resources competed for are nonmaterial; the accumulation of group wealth is frowned on. No group is supposed to keep more in its treasury than a "prudent reserve" for rent and other small expenses.

Dissent may arise from ideological differences—for instance, the inclusion or omission of religious or spiritual components in meetings or from substantial socioeconomic or life-style variations among group members. Sometimes a group may become so big that members feel they must compete for a chance to have their opinions heard, as there is not enough time in the meeting period to allow everyone who wishes a chance to speak. This can lead to dissatisfaction, loss of members, and perhaps the formation of a new group.

Although it is both a national and international movement, A.A. emphasizes decentralization and has only a minimal number of administrative personnel. In contrast to many non-12-step self-help groups that have created large professional national and regional staffs and seek to exert a good deal of control over local chapters, A.A.'s national office provides materials and interacts with pertinent groups on the national scene but exercises little control over the functioning of local units. Nationally, A.A. consists of thousands of cells, meetings, or groups—and it is recognized and appreciated that each cell is different, even unique. As Johnson writes,

> Each meeting is run by the members and each meeting is somewhat different from every other meeting. Some cells . . . are led by charismatic leaders and are fairly rigid, with members required to conform to certain rules and beliefs[;] . . . others are very loosely structured. Some emphasize spirituality (a belief in a "higher power") while in others you may sit through an entire

meeting without hearing the world "alcohol," let alone "God." It is this very structure of A.A., a structure which evolved out of competition (for space, attention, power, prestige, beliefs, and so on) that has allowed A.A. to grow and flourish. . . . If one cannot find a meeting to his or her liking, all s/he needs do is find some other like-minded people and start a new group. (1986, n.p.)


## Birth, Decline, and Dissolution in Groups

Like other organizations, self-help groups may decline in membership, suffer breakaways or defections, or, for various reasons, decide to dissolve. They also may change their focus, the kinds of activities they organize, and even their name, so that they represent their modified program more accurately. Until 1990 there was no empirical research to confirm or challenge the prevalent assumption that changes, membership decline, and dissolution occur in self-help groups. Fortunately, we now have a careful study of the birth and death of self-help groups sponsored by the New Jersey Self-Help Clearinghouse, which maintains an up-to-date, comprehensive computerized listing of all the groups in the state.[5]

The researchers collected growth, birth, mortality, and prevalence data for (a) independent groups (those not affiliated with any national or regional parent organization); (b) A.A., which dwarfs in size all other groups in the state; and (c) all other (i.e., non-A.A.) groups affiliated with a national or regional organization (The Compassionate Friends, Parents Anonymous, etc.).

Findings indicate that (a) the rate at which new groups were being formed in 1983–84 in New Jersey was twice the rate at which they were disbanding, (b) independent groups had a significantly higher growth rate than affiliated groups, and (c) A.A. had a much lower mortality rate than both independent and affiliated groups. Tentative conclusions drawn from the findings were that self-help groups in general and independent groups in particular were steadily increasing in number, that there was a high yearly turnover of groups, and that only for A.A. groups did affiliation with a parent organization appear to have obvious benefits in terms of group survival.

In 1983–84 self-help groups had a growth rate in New Jersey of 10.1 percent. This represented an increase of self-help groups in the state from 2,582 in 1983 to 2,843 in 1984, a net gain of 261 groups. The net growth resulted from two underlying trends that moved in opposite directions: the development of 453 new groups and the disbanding of 192 groups. Thus new groups were developing at a rate of 17.5 percent, more than twice the 7.4 percent rate at which existing groups were disbanding. When the study was repeated to cover 1987 activity, the findings about birth and dissolution rates were very similar.

## Ideology and Rituals

A significant variable among self-help groups is that of the importance and implementation of their ideological principles and beliefs. A continuum can be traced in groups ranging from those with strict, developed, and explicit ideological beliefs and practices to those in which ideology is absent and there is little standardization of what members are expected to believe in and do.

Such groups as A.A. and Recovery, Inc., have well-worked-out sets of beliefs and practices: they expect ideological acceptance or at least acquiescence and lay down behavior codes for members. These are not only connected with the addiction or other problem the group is combatting; they extend to the general realm of personal and social behavior.

As we have seen, meetings of 12-step "anonymous" groups are structured; they usually ascribe to a ritualistic activity sequence: leaders begin meetings by reciting a part of the creed; a speaker is introduced who uses as a text one of the accepted writings or "steps"; the meeting is then turned over to the floor, where members identify themselves as compulsive drinkers, overeaters, gamblers, and so forth and briefly recount their progress and vicissitudes since the last meeting.

Recovery, Inc. chapter meetings follow a different scenario but are also rather standardized. After hearing a speaker or an excerpt from the writings of the group's founder, Dr. Abraham Low, members describe an incident or behavior that has given them difficulty. The group analyzes this offering using Dr. Low's terms and ideas and thereby seeks to have members reinterpret or perceive the difficulty in a different and more acceptable way. These meeting procedures undoubtedly help many members of the groups; they receive positive reinforcement for their abstinence or are aided in accepting and interpreting difficulties they have encountered since the last meeting.

The kind of interactions group members have in meetings may be circumscribed by both the organization's belief system and the centralized procedures established for expression. Spontaneity may be limited. Some 12-step group meetings discourage "cross-talk." Such limitations can be regarded as one of the group's mechanisms for maintaining its cohesion and for tying members more closely to it.

Contrasting with the highly ideologized 12-step organizations are those that have no strong set of enforced beliefs and procedures. These may range from a group like Parents without Partners, which brings together people in a similar life situation but has no stated or explicit ideology, to groups associated with the women's movement, which embrace a wide range and diversity of ideological currents. The styles of such organizations seem freer and more open to individual variation and influence than do the 12-step types. The content of meetings is determined by the participants' desires. The meetings do not follow a set format—there is little stereotyping and consequently more spontaneity and variation.

Another ideology-related difference concerns how long members are expected to remain so. Tightly structured groups modeled on A.A. expect members to remain for life and never to "graduate" to the wider world; one of A.A.'s tenets can be paraphrased as "once a drinker, always a drinker." Reliable control of the addiction can be assured only through confessions of powerlessness, the help of a Higher Power, and continued contact with the group through attending meetings. Even if members have stayed away for a long time, they are welcomed back and considered life-long members.

Nonideological groups like Parents without Partners and those for widowed persons have different attitudes toward continuation. They accept the idea that as members' circumstances change, they may need or desire no further group contacts. These rather basic differences in ideological commitments also are closely related to the structure and dynamics of the various groups' development, to the kinds of participation they evoke, and the benefits that members seem to obtain from them.

An aspect of ideology that significantly influences group development is the group activities and directions that members most value. For example, some members will view the intimacy and interaction of the small group as its major value; others will see growth in size and recognition, success in fund-raising and obtaining government grants, and so forth as major indicators of the group's effectiveness. Such differences of hopes and expectations regarding the group's direction can be disruptive in self-help groups and can even lead to their disintegration.

In a study of feminist organizations, some of which were formed along classic self-help lines, Stephanie Riger found that groups whose members valued independence, participation, and solidarity remained small and intimate. In contrast, groups where efficiency and getting financial help from outside sources were most valued tended to become bureaucratic and to lose the self-help spirit in which they had been founded.[6]

Another variable related to ideology may profoundly affect members' perceptions and satisfactions: the degree of professionals' activity in groups they may have formed or helped to form. Parents Anonymous mandates the presence of a professional at all group meetings in which members' personal problems are the primary focus. This requirement reflects the view that professionals may have greater ability to deal with child-abuse issues than lay group members. In contrast, many non-12-step groups reject the continual involvement of professionals as ideologically incompatible with self-help philosophy and organizational structure.

## Chapter 7

# Relations between Self-Help Groups and Professionals

One of the most complex and controversial topics regarding self-help groups is their existing, desirable, and possible relationships with professionals and human-services agencies. Human-services professionals and self-helpers doubtlessly share the same broad goals of improving the life situations, the functioning, and the morale of those they serve. The differences between them do not arise from overall intentions but from concepts of how best to carry out those goals.

## The Relationship's History

Most of the problems for which self-help groups are formed have to do with human suffering—the need for both material and emotional support by sick or needy people and their relatives; by the elderly, single parents, widowed persons, and many other people experiencing stressful personal troubles, isolation, loneliness, low self-esteem, and feelings of helplessness. If all the social and human-services programs were functioning well and equitably, these problems might not affect so many people, and the formation of self-help groups would be unnecessary.

Some professionals believe in fact that a "welfare-state" society can and should be able to organize comprehensive services for the population and thus obviate the organization of informal services on the self-help model. Some American and British professionals and academics have claimed that "natural helping networks," including self-help groups, are outdated anachronisms, no longer useful or necessary.[1] Others suggest that professionals should concentrate their attention and efforts in direct work with the most needy and vulnerable clients and should not be concerned with the self-organization of clients in mutual-aid groups.[2]

These views, however, seem quite unrealistic. The last 10 to 12 years have witnessed massive cutbacks in the human-services programs of most welfare-state societies, and the attainment of a comprehensive social-services program in even the most advanced modern societies seems at present a rather utopian dream. But even if it were attainable, the prospect of a comprehensive services system for everyone in need is undesirable because it would ignore two of the most important factors in the rise of self-help groups: the need for being part of a community and the importance of self-activity, self-reliance, and self-management.

Self-help groups have flourished in the past few decades because, at least in part, professional care systems have tended to monopolize definitions, diagnoses, and treatment of the problems people face. Because of this tendency professionals have deemphasized their clients' self-understanding, self-management, and self-reliance and have thus fostered dependency and passivity. Some professional programs have been notably ineffective—as in the treatment of alcoholism and other addictions—and the formation of self-help groups such as A.A. has been a natural consequence. In other cases professionals have simply had too little experience with certain problems to understand their nature and circumstances, and self-help groups have been created both to fill the vacuum and to force professional concern with the problem. Professionals have also tended to downplay or overlook the need for community, which involves identification and interaction with a like-minded population of fellow sufferers. In self-help groups such populations learn from each other, overcome isolation, and achieve through collective action what is unattainable by lone individuals or families.

These manifestations have presented human-services professionals with major dilemmas and conflicts: not only has their claimed exclusivity in diagnosing and expertly treating particular problems been revealed to be sometimes exaggerated or hollow, but many people who have joined self-help groups as an alternative to professional care have found the groups effective and satisfying. These developments conflict with what most professionals have been trained to believe: that they have a unique competence and special mission and status. It is therefore no wonder that the professional literature of various human-services fields should have so wide a range of opinion relating to the growing prominence of self-help groups. What professionals have considered their exclusive domain they now have to share with uncredentialed, untrained individuals who, nonetheless, appear to be successfully competing for the same pool of clients/patients.

Not all professionals and agencies have been disturbed by the self-help phenomenon, however. Some have been sympathetic to self-help groups and in various ways have helped these groups with ideas and contacts. Some have even provided material resources, such as a place to meet, telephone, and clerical services. A few professionals have been influential in starting groups: for example, psychiatrist Abraham Low founded Recovery, Inc., and social worker Leonard Lieber co-founded Parents Anonymous.

Self-help researchers Morton Lieberman and Leonard Borman were so impressed by examples of individual professional initiatives in founding self-help groups that they believed this to be more the rule than the exception. In reporting, in 1977, on 10 organizations, most of them national in scope, they found six that were founded by professionals and others where professionals were involved at an early phase of group organization.[3]

While accurate, Lieberman and Borman's findings were based on quite selective instances, however. A good deal of evidence advanced by other scholars refutes the claim that a majority of groups were founded by interested, sympathetic professionals. In a study of the very active self-help scene in Canada, Jean-Marie Romeder found that "more than 70 percent of 200 organizations studied were initiated by lay persons."[4] Similarly, Zachary Gussow and George Tracy, writing about the United States, observe, "Without exception, the prime movers in the establishment of self-help health groups have been patients."[5]

In an early-1980s telephone survey of self-help leaders in upstate New York, Ronald Toseland and Lynda Hacker found that professionals were involved in forming 24 of the 43 groups contacted (56 percent).[6] In New Jersey, in the same period, Edward Madara and Camille Grish found a lower percentage—professionals had helped to start 31 of 67 groups, or 47 percent.[7]

In my 1961 survey of groups formed by parents of handicapped children, I found that no more than half of these groups were formed with any kind of involvement by professionals. The preceding studies suggest that the same ratio holds true for present-day self-help groups.

## How Self-Help Groups and Professionals
## Perceive Each Other

Limited contact with each other often affects how professionals perceive self-help groups and vice versa. Recent studies have shown that professionals were familiar with and could name from three to six community self-help groups and had had personal contact with one or two of them. Considering the great number and diversity of self-help groups, professionals' personal experience with self-help groups, although certainly increasing, is thus still limited. Often the experience and knowledge is confined to groups that work in the particular field of the professional's concern—for instance, A.A or other 12-step groups for professionals working with addicted clients, Mended Hearts for cardiologists and cardiac nurses.

Self-help-group members often have a similarly restricted view of professionals—doctors, nurses, social workers, and so forth—based on personal encounters in a treatment program. Much of the material published by self-help groups deals with such encounters with professionals, and this group literature certainly influences members' attitudes.

Robert Emerick has studied 104 local self-help groups of formerly hospitalized mentally ill persons unaffiliated with such national organizations as Recovery, Inc., GROW, and the NAMI.[8] The "hundreds, even thousands of more moderate and more radical groups" he studied "account for much of the growth within the national self-help movement and constitute more than 35 percent of all groups of former mental patients." According to Emerick, many such groups "were formed to counteract problems that members believe are caused by society or the mental health system. Such groups are extremely conscious of the potential co-optation by professionals." He found that "the largest proportion of groups in the sample, 42.8 percent (36 out of 84), hold anti-professional attitudes, while only 26.2 percent (22 out of 84) are pro-professionals, and 30.9 percent (26 out of 84) are neutral. The strong anti-professional bias of this sample reflects the history of the anti-psychiatry movement since the early 1960s. Despite current indications of moderation within the mental patient movement, former-patient groups are clearly more negative than positive in their attitudes toward mental health professionals" (Emerick, 403).

In my 1961 study, *Parents of the Handicapped*, I interviewed and corresponded with human-services professionals to discern their attitudes toward self-help groups. A professional in a medium-sized Eastern city made these comments about self-help groups in his community:

> Each of these groups is a parents' movement . . . or a cause, if you will. All of them are highly charged with emotion, and with all the identification that takes place when a group of people with a common problem get together. We believe this emotional identification of one parent with the rest, this universality of experience . . . is the driving force behind these organizations. They all have a terrific amount of zeal and momentum, and it seems to have its origin in this fundamental group bond that comes from the shared experience of being parents to severely handicapped children. Much of this attitude seems to originate in the experience these parents have had in the past with schools, social and health agencies, hospitals, doctors and all the rest.
>
> The leaders of each of these organizations are very aggressive people with a terrific amount of drive and consecration to the cause. They embody all the emotional charge and the zeal of their respective groups. They have a peculiar singleness of purpose, and seemingly boundless energy, enthusiasm and time for the cause.
>
> Similarly and finally, none of these groups is content to stand still and each wants to forge ahead toward a continually larger and more elaborate program operation. They have a terrific sense of missionary purpose, and their expansionist ideas are apt to be almost without limit. (1961, 128)

Of 14 professionals surveyed in my 1961 study, two had highly positive attitudes toward self-help groups; five had generally positive attitudes, with some criticisms; four had mixed attitudes, leaning slightly to the negative; and three had generally negative attitudes.

Rita Black and Diane Drachman's 1985 study of hospital social workers' attitudes toward self-help groups found that "workers generally view self-help groups as helpful and report an awareness of an average of over three problem areas or diseases for which groups are available. . . . Respondents' interest in and positive evaluations of self-help groups seemed to have developed out of their recognition of the needs of their clients."[9]

Nancy Bryant studied 211 members of several professional disciplines working in hospitals in the San Diego area. She concluded that "generally speaking, most hospital professionals viewed community self-help groups in a positive light. . . . Only 10 percent of the respondents felt that self-help group members . . . abandon all professional advice and help. Another small minority, 2 percent, did not perceive self-help groups as a valuable form of treatment. . . . However some 23 percent of these hospital professionals did indicate some concern about the lack of professional guidance in self-help meetings."[10]

In a large study Leon Levy mailed questionnaires to several hundred mental-health professionals nationwide and found positive attitudes: 84 percent of respondents believed the self-help groups they were familiar with to be of at least "average effectiveness"; 47 percent believed that self-help groups could play an "important or very important role" in improving community mental-health programs.[11]

Research has also occasionally targeted the perceptions and attitudes of self-help-group members toward professionals. Linda Kurtz surveyed the attitudes of A.A. and substance-abuse-program leaders toward the interactions their members had with various professionals. She found that "the A.A. members complained of infrequent contact, a lack of understanding about A.A. policies with respect to professionals, and the use of disapproved interventions in substance abuse programs, for example, medication."[12] In Toseland and Hacker's 1982 telephone interview study, a number of self-help leaders expressed unhappiness with professionals' lack of understanding and inappropriate behavior toward them.

## Professionals' Views

**The Possible Dangers in Self-Help Groups**  The concern of some professionals that certain characteristics of self-help groups may be hazardous to the individual's well-being is by no means new, but the volume of critical commentary on this issue has swelled considerably, quite in keeping with the enormous increase in professional/self-help interaction.

Professionals are often fearful that self-help groups will create or intensify emotional problems that the group's lay members are not equipped to deal with. A physician may worry that the technical information acquired by his/her patients and their families could be conveyed inappropriately and inaccurately at self-help-group meetings to others who are dealing with a similar medical problem. Some professionals fear that group members may spread misinformation and encourage others to adopt quack remedies or simplistic "solutions" to a complicated problem—"solutions" that could very well intensify the sufferer's depression and pain when he/she realizes that the remedy is ineffective.

A related danger often expressed by health-field professionals is that some group leaders who read widely in technical and professional literature come to regard themselves as professionals in their own right, fully capable of dealing with technical issues; they will thereby discourage group members from consulting with qualified professionals in situations of need.

Professionals also fear that groups may encourage their members to shop around, to compare the performance and values of facilities and personnel available, and in so doing to reflect adversely on, even to threaten, the reputations and status of respected professionals.

It is apparent that these criticisms stem from the groups' challenge to the monopolistic position and self-perceptions of professionals and established institutions in the community.

**What the Relationship Should Be**   Given all these contentious issues, it is natural that various ideas will have been advanced by both professionals and self-help groups to resolve the continuing relationship problems. Alan Gartner and Frank Riessman proposed in 1980 that self-help groups and mental-health professionals were "made for each other" in that they have the same purposes and do essentially identical work.[13] Derived from this viewpoint is the idea that the present discord is the product of each side's ignorance of the other and of the goals and methods they share. Educating each side about the other and heightening interactions between them is seen as the solution.

Another formula for improved relations is for both sides to recognize that they are "two wings of the same bird"—that is, that both kinds of help are needed to help individuals and families solve their problems. Although these two approaches appear attractive and seem plausible on the surface, both seem inadequate in their concept of the relationship and in guiding its improvement.

Gartner and Riessman's formulation implies that self-help groups and professionals do the same things for clients or members, and that they are therefore more or less interchangeable. This idea breaks down as soon as we take into account the peer group influence and the sense of community generated by self-help groups. A professional usually is not a "peer" in the sense of having a personal experience with the problem. Nor can a professional's contact with a client provide group identification and a sense of belonging to a community.

The idea that both kinds of helping service are needed by troubled individuals or families also does not seem accurate or useful. In some situations self-help groups alone are very effective; in others technical professional knowledge is the first requisite. Even if both forms of service are required, they may be needed successively, not simultaneously.

Research has shown a substantive difference in what professionals and self-help groups do and in the processes group members expect and value from the organization and the meetings they attend. The authors of one study, for example, conclude that, in contrast to professional approaches,

> from what self-help group members say, elegant theoretical formulations, systematic behavioral techniques and complex cognitive re-structuring are not essential components of change. What is essential for change is meeting a core of personal and social needs—needs for constructive advice, empathic communication, acceptance, self-expression and understanding and for developing an enhanced sense of personal responsibility, hope, control and self-worth. In view of the broad scope, rapid proliferation, and huge membership of self-help groups, human services professionals would be wise to give these needs foremost consideration. (Wollert et al., 215)

In addition to studies of mutual perceptions and attitudes of professionals and self-help-group members there have been studies that compare the processes of groups dealing with the same problem when they are led by professionals and when they are led by lay members. Yoak and Chesler studied 43 groups organized by the Candlelighters, a self-help group formed by parents of children with various types of cancer, and found that

> the professionally led groups were significantly less formal, smaller, and younger, did not as often involve parents of deceased children, and stressed emotional support activities. . . . [T]he professionally led groups were not as often engaged in such active functions as promoting changes in the system of medical care or providing outreach to newly diagnosed families.
>
> Professionally led groups . . . focus on emotional support, on sharing and ventilating feelings to alleviate the stresses of their children's illness. The more diverse—and often more task-oriented—activities of the parent-led groups may reflect the wider range of needs and priorities parents themselves see—perhaps a need to have an impact on the fight against childhood cancer, to make the medical system more humane, or to reach out to other parents and families in their own times of crisis. (1985, 49)

The studies cited make clear what I have emphasized throughout this volume: that what self-help groups do for their participants—what takes place in their meetings—is different in kind from what occurs in contacts with professionals and institutions. The self-help experience is unique, a fact that all people concerned with human-services programs must recognize and appreciate.

## Government Recognition

We have reached a new stage not only in professional/self-help-group relations but in government recognition of the importance of self-help groups as legitimate components of human-services programs. A watershed event in the self-help field was the September 1987 Workshop on Self-Help and Public Health convened by the former surgeon-general, Dr. C. Everett Koop. The workshop's 175 invitees comprised a wide spectrum of individuals from five major categories: the self-help movement, including self-help clearinghouses and a range of local and national self-help groups with a health orientation; functionaries from relevant federal, state, and local government agencies; business and industry; private foundations with a possible interest in financing self-help activities and research; and academics who have contributed to the study and analysis of self-help groups. Professional organizations represented were the American Medical Association, the American Hospital Association, and the National League of Nursing; national voluntary health agencies included the National March of Dimes and the National Arthritis foundations.

The two major themes of the workshop were (a) How can the health of the public be improved through partnership between self-help and the health-care delivery system? and (b) How can these partnerships be achieved without compromising the essential nature of self-help? A series of recommendations were developed through extensive small group discussions of these and related issues. Surgeon-General Koop's closing speech reviewed the general recommendations and the following specific ones, directed toward his office:

1. Establish a national toll-free telephone number to obtain information regarding groups and for use by individuals, agencies, and state and local clearinghouses.
2. Write letters to all professional schools of health training (medical schools, nursing schools, social work programs, etc.) recommending that they incorporate self-help training, seminars, courses, awareness, etc. Schools should use resources such as self-helpers themselves and the self-help clearinghouse to help promote awareness in these seminars.
3. Develop and deliver generic public service announcements, originating from the office of the surgeon-general regarding self-help, during the

course of the next year. Self-helpers will participate in developing these announcements.

4. When testifying on any health issue, the subject of self-help should be integrated into this testimony.

5. Promote an awareness of self-help in all dealings with professional associations.

6. Encourage, as a matter of public health policy, the inclusion of self-help in any federally funded health service or health promotion programs.[14]

These suggestions were based on the understanding that, through the prestige and visibility of his office, the surgeon-general could personally influence the growth and development of self-help in health as a social movement.

Dr. Koop carried out a number of these recommendations prior to his retirement in June 1989. The 15-member National Council on Self-Help and Public Health was established in 1988 with some government funding, and it carries out education and research and liaison contacts with federal government officials. These activities have social movement aspects, as they reflect a common ideology, an organizational structure, and an interest in social change—that is, changing the attitudes of the public, professionals, educators, and government functionaries toward self-help.

## Toward a Synthesis

From research cited in this and other chapters, it is clear that self-help groups have been created spontaneously by lay people and also to some extent by interested, informed, and sympathetic professionals. The number of the latter is growing, and the knowledge and acceptance of self-help groups by professionals in the various clinical fields is far greater than it was one or two decades ago.[15] I must emphasize nevertheless that the self-help "movement" has been chiefly a self-starting, spontaneous, grass-roots phenomenon that has created its own culture, its own traditions, its own work methods, and its own structures. As indicated by the research cited, self-help groups organized and conducted by lay people have a somewhat different character and function differently from those created and led by professionals.

It is now acknowledged by many professionals who have had contacts with them that self-help groups, both of the 12-step and non-12-step variety, provide several key factors that professional services cannot: the powerful element of peer support, the effects of individual role models in the group, and the interactions occasioned by the giving and receiving of help. Other factors that distinguish self-help-group meetings from professional encounters lie in the socialization of the group experience: groups are close to the give-and-take of everyday life, they are concerned with the present, and they facilitate spontaneous personal relationships. There is growing appreciation of the fact that professional help, however competent, sensitive, and well-meaning, does not and cannot supply these qualities.

It is also true that while many professionals and agencies are now more positive about self-help groups, make referrals to them, and provide them with information and occasionally consultation and material resources, there is still a long way to go before professionals broadly accept these groups and a full and mutually beneficial working partnership develops.

The January 1988 issue of *Psychology Today* (a publication of the American Psychological Association) carried several articles on self-help groups—some favorable, some critical, but overall disparaging and patronizing. The magazine concluded that if they accept the guidance of professional psychologists, "self-help groups *may* became legitimate and accepted parts of mental health services."[16] Such a comment in a publication of the chief professional organization of psychologists would hardly sit well with the thousands of members of Recovery, Inc., GROW, A.A., and other 12-step groups, who believe that they are and have been for some time "legitimate" parts of mental-health services and that legitimacy is not conferred by professionals but decided on by the consumers of services.

As we have seen, some professionals fear they will lose their monopoly in patient diagnosis and treatment to the lay persons who constitute self-help groups. Their resistance and fears have an economic basis as well: "turf" problems arise from the situation that, according to the National Association of Social Workers, 50 percent of trained social workers in the United States have a full- or part-time private practice; the ratio for clinical psychologists is undoubtedly higher.[17] Revenue-wise, self-help groups may seem to be diminishing the pool of troubled people that professional practitioners hope to attract.

At a 1989 follow-up meeting to the surgeon-general's landmark 1987 workshop, I discussed some principles and methods for self-help education in the professional fields:

It is necessary to have materials in professional curricula that show in fact what *lay people know, what they can do for themselves, what lay self-help groups can accomplish for patients and their families,* and that also show that true professionalism involves respect for and partnership with these lay resources. One way of doing this is to build into professional education at many levels the participation of former and present patients and their organization—in classes, in field contacts, even in research studies. A few medical educators are doing just that—I think particularly of Dr. Merrijoy Kelner, of the University of Toronto —and I hope such an approach is penetrating social work, public health and nursing education, too.[18]

While such curricular additions are important, they would not affect the many already-trained professionals practicing in the community. Changing some of the attitudes and practice is a big task of unlearning or relearning, similar to the way industrial workers must learn new skills when their plants begin making different products. Professionals have difficulty comprehending that education is a two-way street. Self-help-group participants learn not from books or classes but from often hard and bitter experiences, and such knowledge should be made available to professionals as a prime component of their understanding of people's problems.

Through contact with self-help groups professionals will learn that one of the most important issues for group participants is that of ownership. The greatest threat that professionals, institutions, and agencies pose to self-help groups is that of co-optation, of taking them over. Group members may welcome professional help but be afraid of losing control of what they have worked so hard to build. In my 1989 paper I stated, "Professionals must learn to evaluate their own motives and actions in working with groups to make sure that, consciously or unconsciously, they are not pushing toward takeover, perhaps in the interest of what they see as efficiency" (1989, 61).

It seems certain that we will see more contact between professionals and self-help groups, greater cooperation and research toward social-problem solutions, and enhanced respect for the special knowledge and experience that each side possesses, while appreciating their differences. In short, a mutually respectful partnership, with acceptance of legitimacy and uniqueness on both sides, seems the desirable way ahead.

*Chapter 8*

# Populism and Social Action in Self-Help Groups

In some important nineteenth-century social movements—trade unions, among others—self-help principles were prominent both in these groups' organization and in serving their members' needs. Similarly, self-help groups of this century have found that engaging in sociopolitical actions to effect policy changes that will benefit members and nonmembers alike is important not only for the ends achieved but also because the social action becomes a unifying force for the group. This chapter focuses jointly on (a) the embodiment of some self-help principles and methods in popular, grass-roots organizations and (b) the political and social actions of non-12-step self-help groups.

## Populist Organizations in the United States

A popular but largely forgotten organization of the nineteenth century—and one incorporating both self-help philosophy and practices—was the Ladies Physiological Society, which originated in Boston in the 1840s and soon expanded rapidly to other cities. The society's initial focus was women's health interests—pregnancy, childbirth, and child rearing. According to one history of nineteenth-century health reform,

> Health reform struck a responsive chord in . . . enthusiastic female audiences. The lecture halls were filled with women eager for the knowledge

they hoped would ease their bewilderment with their increased responsibilities within the family—at a time when the home was plagued by pressures imposed from without, by a mobile, fragmented, and fast-changing society.
. . .

   Health reform offered to countless women a means of coping with an imprecise, undependable, and often hostile environment. In a society in which women were expected to play an increasingly complex role in the nurture of children and the organization of family life, health reform brought to the bewildered housewife not just sympathy and compassion but a structured regimen, a way of life. Women were promised a means to end their isolation and make contact with others of their sex. . . . A deep sense of sisterhood was evidenced.[1]

The Ladies Physiological Society campaigned and educated women to promote better nutrition and self-care during pregnancy, including the wearing of less-restrictive clothing, "natural" childbirth in the home, and the rearing of infants and toddlers according to folk wisdom, which diverged from the prevailing repressive medical and religious dictates. The society not only advised women on their day-to-day behavior, but it also dispensed a philosophy that paralleled that of contemporary feminism: "Acknowledging the positive influence of women in society and the family led . . . to a re-examination of the relationship between the sexes. During these years many . . . openly rejected the older authoritarian concept of marriage in favor of a relationship based on mutual love, common interests, and affection" (Morantz, 87).
   Self-help principles and methods were likewise embodied in other kinds of nineteenth-century political and social organizations that constituted what is generally referred to as the American populist movement. Before the Civil War populist organizations were created in particular by farmers and rural populations and among small merchants in the towns. Their overall objective was to build resistance to political domination by the federal government in Washington and to the economic power of big business, banks, and other financial institutions. To do this, farmers set up cooperatives for both production and distribution of their goods, offering economies in obtaining loans, purchasing equipment, and marketing their products. From local activities, a strong national body was formed to promote these cooperative initiatives: the national Farmers Alliance and Industrial Union. Lawrence Goodwyn writes of this populist organization, "By the time the alliance had grown to two million members, largely concentrated in twenty states in the South and West, the participants had learned a number of rather elemental lessons in a democratic conduct."[2]

These initially economic-based populist organizations parallel what takes place in self-help groups formed around a single condition or issue. As Goodwyn writes, "Perhaps the most significant institution of the Populists—one that they came to learn from their own organizing experience in democratic movement building—is that once people agree to work together for an agreed-upon goal, the experience of working toward that objective has the effect of raising their sights by transforming their understanding" (Goodwyn, 26–27).

This consciousness transformation among cooperative members led the organizations to the political arena. As local and regional groups flourished, they coalesced, and some became national in scope. Dissatisfaction with and lack of confidence in the two main political parties climaxed after the Civil War, and in 1892 various populist organizations formed the People's party, which, though it campaigned vigorously, was unsuccessful and disintegrated in 1896. Despite this failure, however, the populist movement was strongly committed to electoral politics, its influence peaking with the presidential campaigns of William Jennings Bryan in 1890 and Wisconsin Senator Robert La Follette in 1924.

Cornel West has aptly summarized the nature and contributions of American populism in the nineteenth century:

> The strengths of populism constitute the best of the democratic tradition of a rural, preindustrial, pastoral America: local control, decentralized economic relations, small-scale political institutions, limited property ownership, and intimate, face-to-face interaction and association. This important stress on local activism, politics of everyday life of ordinary people, and discernible, credible, and visible forms of people's empowerment is rooted in homespun American ideologies of Jeffersonian and Jacksonian civil republicanism.[3]

To this short list we should add populism's opposition to bureaucracy, to government's and other power sources' impersonal and alienating practices.

Complex, multiple social forces revived the traditions of populism in American society after World War II in what has come to be know as the "new populism." As a result of President Lyndon B. Johnson's War on Poverty in the 1960s, there sprang up thousands of local, grass-roots citizen-action organizations that followed the principles and methods put forth by Saul Alinsky. During this period and after, some strong coalitions and federations were created to work on national problems such as poverty, homelessness, unemployment caused by plant closings, racial discrimination, and health care.

These developments were greatly stimulated by Congress's passage of President Johnson's Economic Opportunity Act in 1964, of which Robert Fisher writes,

> The most innovative and central feature of the legislation and one that most emphasized the ideals of "maximum feasible participation" and local control was the Community Action Program (CAP). The program established Community Action Agencies (CAAs) to sponsor neighborhood self-help projects, promote social action, mobilize local resources, and coordinate local programs. These CAAs would address concerns heretofore left to city, state, and nationwide organizations, and would be directly supported by public funds, 90 percent of which would come from the federal government. If the city or town refused to put up the 10 percent seed money or in-kind payment, then private groups could do so. The program spread like a prairie fire. Within eighteen months of the passage of the OEO legislation there were over 1,000 funded CAAs in the United States. While CAAs differed dramatically depending on the local political environment, the fights for citizen participation and for neighborhood organizing dominated the first years of most locals.[4]

Responding to events of the 1960s and the severe economic recession at the time, this interest in neighborhood organizing accelerated all over the United States in the 1970s. More than 20 million Americans were said to have been active in hundreds of thousands of neighborhood groups. Several thousand block clubs were reported in New York City alone. The National Commission on Neighborhoods listed more than 8,000 local community-action groups nationwide. Communities Organized for Public Service (COPS) of San Antonio, Texas, one of the largest single community organizations in the nation, had 6,000 delegates to its 1976 convention, only two years after it began. Ten years after its creation in 1980, the Association of Community Organizations for Reform Now (ACORN) claimed 25,000 active, dues-paying members in its neighborhood organizations in 19 states (Fisher, 116).

## Consumerism

A different form and focus of populist expression was also increasingly evident in the same period: consumerism. Many organizations were created to combat high prices, monopolistic price-fixing, shoddy workmanship, "planned obsolescence," and the marketing of hazardous products. In contrast to earlier consumer movements, these groups could provide scientific and technical analysis of widely publicized products, as seen in the various organizations created by or associated with Ralph Nader. Media exposure and public education helped bring about a higher level of consumer consciousness than had previously existed.

The present-day consumer movement had some of its most notable and successful activities and effects in the field of health care and health products. Health-oriented self-help groups are, as I have discussed earlier, prominent and numerous: mutual-aid groups of patients exist for almost all of the 200 major disease categories analyzed by the World Health Organization. Groups formed by those other than patients (i.e., by parents or other caretakers of sick or disabled persons) are also numerous and growing rapidly.

Many of the health-related self-help groups have adopted or developed a consumerist stance. Some groups, as I have noted, arose because of members' dissatisfaction with the care they received from health-care professionals or with these people's understanding of the problem. These groups were established at least partly to obtain for their members more attention from physicians and other professionals and better care.

At the 1989 symposium Self-Help and the Impact of Life-Threatening Conditions, Fitzhugh Mullan, director of the U.S. Public Health Service's Bureau of Health Professions, stated,

> Another self-help group theme is consumerism. There is a lot of consumerism in what we are doing but we ought to think a little more about this. Look at the National Consumers League and look at consumer reports; look at groups that have gotten down the last bit of strategy for how to buy an icebox. We should be equally clear on how to pick a physician or how to pick a psychotherapist, or how to select orthodox and non-orthodox treatments, etc. Elements of consumerism include our relationship to professionals, as consumers, as patients and as clients. This relationship should be quality-monitored.[5]

Health-oriented groups raise the consumer consciousness of their members in several ways. First, they evaluate institutions and individual professionals according to the care and knowledge of the problem they offer. Much discussion of the best place to obtain specific services goes on at self-help-group meetings. Second, they evaluate the cost and effectiveness of products on the market—drugs, appliances, diets, exercise programs, and so forth. Third, they often deal with legislative policy issues, joining with consumer activists and other citizen groups to support or oppose particular legislation or policy proposals.

## Policy Advocacy

One of the most impressive examples of older populist social actions by self-help groups was the Pennsylvania Association for Retarded Children's long campaign in the early 1970s to obtain integrated (with nonhandicapped students) and thereby better public education for their children. The Pennsylvania parents' organization eventually went to court and won judgments that resulted in greatly improved public school facilities, and parent self-help groups in other states followed this example. The Pennsylvania parents work was a major stimulus to Congress in passing the landmark Education for All Handicapped Act of 1974 (Public Law 92-146), which guarantees all children with physical or mental disabilities living in the community the right to public education.

At about the same time that parents of retarded children won their campaigns for integrated schooling, a group of hemophilia sufferers waged a protracted and successful battle to get federal subsidies for the blood and blood derivative products hemophiliacs need. Spearheading this campaign was the National Hemophilia Foundation, a self-help group founded in 1950 with chapters in every state. Meeting similar success were local and national self-help groups of end-stage renal (kidney disease) patients and their relatives: these groups' lobbying efforts resulted in Congress's 1972 mandate that hemodialysis be federally funded. These examples illustrate the role of health-related self-help groups in organizing sociopolitical pressure to create new facilities or to guaranteed government funding of effective but costly treatment programs.

A somewhat different emphasis is found in groups that campaign to change or enforce existing laws to deal with a particular problem. One of the most rapidly growing self-help groups is Mothers against Drunk Driving (MADD), which has succeeded in getting several states to stiffen drunk driver prosecutions and penalties. Self-help groups have also been politically active in the area of occupational health and environmental hazards: non-self-help environmental organizations have joined such groups as the Black Lung Association in its campaign to improve coalmine ventilation and Emphysema Anonymous in its fight against air pollutants.

As noted in earlier chapters, the National Alliance for the Mentally Ill not only works on the psychological and community problems of discharged patients and their families but also campaigns for better day-care and community outpatient facilities, improved conditions in state mental hospitals, and employment and training services for former patients. The NAMI has been given major credit for the National Institute of Mental Health's 1989–90 budget being the largest allotment in the institute's history.

The National Council of Independent Living Centers (NCILC) is a national coalition of some 200 local self-help organizations of persons with disabilities. It has effectively campaigned for improved procedures for disabled social security recipients, for the recruitment of personal attendants for disabled persons who need them, for making public transportation facilities wheelchair accessible, for housing adaptations, and for the opening up of jobs for persons with disabilities. The group's greatest achievement—and one of the most important examples of social action by self-help groups—is unquestionably its late-1980s campaign that led to in passage of the Americans with Disabilities Act (ADA), which President George Bush signed into law in July 1990 and which went into effect in July 1992.

The ADA prohibits private-sector discrimination and covers employment, public services and accommodations, transportation, and communication. A business employing more than 25 people, for instance, cannot refuse to hire a qualified disabled applicant if the person can do the work with "reasonable accommodations." Hotels, restaurants, and other private businesses must, the ADA mandates, eliminate architectural barriers if such changes are "readily available"; businesses must make "reasonable accommodations" to offer goods and services to the disabled, unless the accommodations would cause "undue burdens." The law requires that buses be accessible to all and that supplemental paratransit services be "comparable" to services for the general public.

NCILC representatives and other self-help organizations of persons with disabilities had worked for several years with members of Congress and their staffs in drafting this comprehensive legislation, which has been called the Magna Carta for the 43 million Americans who have some form of disability. The self-help groups worked just as diligently to secure support for the act's passage from Congress and the Bush administration. These groups and coalitions carried out a tireless national campaign of education, persuasion, lobbying, public demonstrations, and media contacts. Bush's signing of the act was preceded in May and June of 1990 by massive demonstrations in Washington, D.C., and important state capitals that included thousands of people in wheelchairs.

On a much smaller and less dramatic scale, a typical ongoing sociopolitical action by a self-help group is reported by the newsletter of the National Marfan Foundation, an organization of sufferers from Marfan syndrome, a hereditary, mobility-impairing connective-tissue disorder that affects some 30,000 people in the United States. This is from the June 1990 newsletter:

Priscilla Ciccariello, Chair, and Beverley Kiefer, NMF member from Iowa, recently went to Washington, D.C., to testify before the Senate Appropriations Subcommittee on Labor, Health and Human Services, Education and Related Agencies. This Subcommittee, chaired by Senator Tom Harkin (D-IA) is responsible for making recommendations to the Appropriations Committee regarding funding for the National Institutes of Health.

Mrs. Kiefer testified about the critical need for biomedical research at the National Institute of Arthritis, Musculoskeletal and Skin Diseases (NIAMSD) on all heritable disorders of connective tissue, of which Marfan syndrome is one. Mrs. Kiefer, who has several affected children and grandchildren, related her personal experiences which are similar to those of many families with Marfan syndrome. . . .

The National Marfan Foundation has been monitoring the progress of the Pepper Commission and other potential legislation concerning access to health care for all Americans. Because the Marfan syndrome is a genetic condition, many insurance companies classify it as "pre-existing" and refuse coverage. For those companies that do provide coverage, some will cancel it after surgery is necessary, while others will impose a "cap" or charge rates which are unaffordable to most people. It is important that the recommendation of the Pepper Commission be reviewed carefully by members of Congress and that legislation be enacted to make health insurance available to people with the Marfan syndrome and the many other conditions now being denied coverage.[6]

This type of advocacy—testimony before and exerting political pressure on legislators by expressing the needs of the special-interest group—is a common and accepted activity of self-help groups, especially the large number of health-oriented ones. Federal, state, and local officials and politicians have learned to respect both the knowledge and the commitment on behalf of their members of self-help group representatives.

Legislators increasingly hear testimony from and consult with group representatives, as the ADA experience and the Marfan account demonstrate.

It should be noted that in these actions self-help groups frequently do not go it alone but reach out for allies. In organizing support for the passage of the ADA, the NCILC enlisted the aid of professional associations such as the American Rehabilitation Institute and the Sister Kenny Foundation, and also of such popular, grass-roots—though not strictly self-help—organizations as the People's Medical Society. The ADA demonstrations in Washington and state capitals garnered support and participation from many nondisabled members of local citizens' groups.

Similarly, when broad social or political issues or campaigns are organized by citizen-action groups or coalitions, they increasingly turn, for support and assistance, to self-help groups. A broad campaign was organized in California in the spring of 1990 to get on the November ballot a referendum to raise taxes on alcoholic beverages. Because hundreds of thousands of signatures are required to get a referendum on the election-year ballot, organizers of this referendum sought assistance from such California self-help groups as the Independent Living Centers, many of which collected signatures.

Adoption of sociopolitical actions by self-help groups may differ according to the unorthodoxy or militancy of the methods. Most groups would find testimony and letter writing to Congress and gathering signatures perfectly acceptable, though public demonstrations and acts of civil disobedience might not be. Some self-help groups in fact have continuing conflicts regarding how militant their actions should be and whether to cooperate with grass-roots organizations that may be considered too radical.

## Conclusion

From the examples presented of sociopolitical actions, or "advocacy" as it is now often called, it is clear that, in ways that harken back to America's populist tradition, many non-12-step self-help groups engage in various forms of education and pressure, especially on governmental bodies and legislators, the latter of which are seen as more responsive to citizen pressures than are private institutions and agencies. The social-action methods self-help groups use are diverse yet quite similar to those of today's populist, grass-roots groups: education and pressure of politicians through lobbying, public demonstrations, delegations, mass meetings, media coverage, and so forth. Consumer boycotts and lawsuits may occur if the organizations feel that other methods have not been effective. The resemblance of self-help-group sociopolitical action to the activities of grassroots citizen-action groups is not accidental: these groups have a common heritage and interact, exchange methods, learn from each other, and often work jointly on particular issues, as in the well-planned, broad campaign for the Americans with Disabilities Act.

A major segment of the self-help movement—12-step groups—neither believes in nor engages in sociopolitical activities. A.A. and the many other 12-step groups that follow its principles eschew all such actions. A.A.'s 12 traditions specifically prohibit taking a political stand on any public issue; such activity is seen as potentially divisive for a group that should be unified around a single purpose. Thus A.A. takes no position on the sale, advertising, or taxation of liquor, or on state drunk-driving laws, and it supports no political candidates. In reaction to such limitations, a non-12-step organization called SOAR (Society of Americans for Recovery) was formed in 1990 by former Iowa Senator Harold Hughes, a recovering alcoholic. SOAR is conceived as a grass-roots political action group that combats discrimination against alcoholics and other drug-dependent individuals and their families. Some self-help analysts claim that members of A.A. and other 12-step groups support sociopolitical actions as individuals, but this assertion seems very difficult to investigate and to document, and even if it were so, it would not change the basic difference in philosophy between the two types of groups.

Some writers have referred to self-help groups as "prepolitical," suggesting that all such groups have the potential to become sociopolitically active. But this characterization clearly does not apply to A.A. and the other 12-step groups. It seems reasonable to estimate that at at least half of non-12-step groups engage on sociopolitical actions. Many join citizen-action, consumerist, or environmentalist organizations to support political candidates and programs that will benefit society as well as their members. In this way, there is a confluence and continuity between the important populist traditions in American society and the activities of modern self-help groups.

*Chapter 9*

# Self-Help Groups and Public Policy

## Some Basic Issues

Basic questions of social policy arise from the relationships different levels of government—federal, state, and local—can have with self-help groups, some of which have been touched on in Chapter 8 and earlier sections of this book. This chapter considers various actual and possible relationships in greater detail, because they are relevant to the current situation of self-help groups and are likely to become increasingly so in the future. Pertinent to discuss are not only government policies and attitudes toward self-help groups in the United States but also the situation in other countries, where different, and in some ways more developed, policies and relationship patterns are found.

There is inherent dilemma or paradox in the issue of government involvement, summed up by the questions "Isn't government interest and support incompatible with self-help initiatives, which emphasize a group's autonomy and freedom from outside control?" and "Can government be interested in and support self-help groups without at the same time seeking to dominate and control them?" These questions go to the heart of self-help group concerns, since, as we have seen, an important motive for the groups' creation was to avoid or to minimize professional controls. While using the resources and help that professional institutions and personnel can give, self-help groups usually start small, are weak, and lack resources in their early stages; thus they often are able to gain something from the interest of, and contacts with, professionals. Yet the possibility and fear of takeover or cooptation by professionals is widely felt among self-help group leaders and members. They see that professionals can provide a good deal of knowledge, status, and contacts and often some material resources. Professionals who want to help naturally want to use their resources and skills, especially when they see that a group's leaders are inexperienced, often heavily burdened, and even incapacitated at times, so that they cannot function consistently.

The dependency dilemma arises for self-help-group contacts with all outside professionals, but when these professionals are government personnel it becomes more acute. On the one hand, many groups would regard government support and partial financing of their programs as a natural and expected function—something like funding public schools or libraries. On the other hand, however, self-help groups realize that there are always ground rules and restrictions when public money is given—recipients are held accountable, must report back, show that the expenditures they have made were for the expected purposes, and so forth. In short, some kind of monitoring or surveillance would seem to be an inevitable accompaniment of government subsidies to self-help groups.

This potential conflict is continuously debated by self-help organizations in the United States and in many European countries. Can a model be found that would combine government financial support to them with a minimum of reporting back, control, or veto power?

## Self-Help and Government Contacts in the United States

Before the financial issues emerged, however, U.S. self-help groups had for a long time tried to get different levels of government to see self-help as a useful, supplementary way of meeting human problems that government was required by law to deal with. Most of these human problems were in the spheres of physical and mental health, where a continuing government interest and active operational role have long been accepted and implemented. In the 1950s and 1960s, when many health-related self-help groups were founded, they did not often look to government for direct financial aid, although many groups requested that government agencies should subsidize research and education relating to the particular problem.

The first important recognition of a self-help group came in 1962, when, in setting up a National Commission on Mental Illness and Mental Retardation, President John F. Kennedy stated that the Association for

Retarded Children had done more to educate the public about mental retardation than any other agency or group in the United States. Kennedy's tribute to a self-help organization's work was, however, an isolated instance at the time and was not echoed by others in government positions until about 1973. By then the rapid growth, appeal to lay people, and apparent usefulness of self-help groups could not be overlooked by government planners in the health and mental-health fields. At the same time, the steeply rising costs of medical care in both the public and private sectors, plus broadened concepts of the needs of the chronically ill and their families, intensified interest in methods of self-care and in what self-help groups could provide.

Spurred on by these considerations, a number of meetings were organized by different units of the federal government in the mid-1970s to discuss and assess the values of self-help and self-care. The National Institute of Mental Health (NIMH), the Bureau of Health Education of the Centers for Disease Control, and the National Heart, Blood, and Lung Institute organized small meetings of self-help and self-care scholars and proponents in the mid- and late 1970s. General recommendations to include self-help and self-care as legitimate, viable components of good health care emerged from these meetings but were not joined to specific action or budgetary proposals. Larger conferences dealing with self-help's role in genetic disease and in combating drug dependency were organized in Washington by the sickle-cell disease branch of the National Heart, Blood, and Lung Institute in 1982 and by ADAMHA, the NIMH's drug agency branch, in 1983. These conferences were attended by clinical practitioners from the various disciplines working with patients and their families, representatives of pertinent self-help groups, government functionaries, and academic researchers. To self-helpers, these meetings evidenced government recognition of the value of their efforts and organizations, a realization that also strongly influenced other attendees.

The same period—from 1975 to 1985—also saw the organization of a number of state-financed self-help clearinghouses to disseminate information on and promote the growth of self-help groups within the state. The earliest and best known of these clearinghouses were set up in New Jersey, California, New York, Illinois, and Minnesota.

With President Ronald Reagan's 1983 appointment of Dr. C. Everett Koop as U.S. surgeon-general, clearinghouse leaders sought to interest him in self-help. They found that he was broadly knowledgeable and sympathetic to the approach, having in fact organized self-help groups of parents in his earlier clinical work as a pediatric surgeon. Dr. Koop's interest culminated in his sponsorship of the September 1987 Workshop on Self-Help and Public Health, held in Los Angeles. While Dr. Koop's workshop was not followed by any specific federal budgetary commitment to promoting self-help, its recommendations furthered general acceptance of self-help groups as a community treatment resource by federal agencies and specifically heightened their readiness to support self-help research. Thus, in 1989 and 1990, the NIMH established self-help research centers at two prominent state universities—Michigan and California—and research on clinical applications of self-help methods was encouraged and supported by several of the National Institutes of Health.

Clearinghouse support has continued to be offered by some of the more populous states, although at reduced levels, reflecting both budgetary limitations and the belief that, over time, clearinghouses should become self-supporting. Self-help clearinghouses have not been very successful at doing this; without continuing state support a number have had to terminate. There have been suggestions that self-help clearinghouses should be basically financed by the self-help groups in their jurisdiction, but this idea is impractical because most local, state, and even national self-help groups are financially insecure.

## Government Policies and Relationships in Other Countries

Self-help organizations can be found in nearly every industrialized country today, but, as noted in Chapter 1, no other country has anywhere near the number of those in the United States. The reasons for this difference relate to history, national culture and outlook, the degree of urbanization, and especially the comprehensiveness of "welfare-state" provisions. For example, a National Health Care System has existed in Great Britain since 1949, and national health-care insurance is found in all other industrialized countries except South Africa and the United States. As noted earlier, some writers believe such programs reduce or obviate the necessity for self-help groups. Most industrial countries' social security programs are broader than that of the United States, providing coverage against other hazards and life exigencies. For self-help analysts, such differences account for the greater number of self-help groups and participants in this country, where the national ethos is that of depending on oneself and family, not on government, when problems arises. Gustave De Cocq has written on this point:

The American view is predicated on a value orientation that holds the individual and his family responsible for the social ills that befall them. These ills must be cured, alleviated, or ameliorated primarily by the individual himself; by his relatives and friends only to the extent that the individual cannot cope. Society, through its agents in the public sector, may intervene only when other means have failed. If one looks at self-help organizations in North America from this perspective, it is not surprising that they have been essentially individually oriented, have not traditionally secured state or public support, and are considered essentially antithetical to Government ventures. On the other hand, in Western Europe it is held that the social ills befalling the individual arise from a faulty societal structure, thus placing the burden of responsibility for ameliorating or curing these ills on society as a whole. If the phenomenon of self-help is viewed from this perspective, it is not surprising that in Western European countries much of the self-help undertaking is not only sanctioned by Government, but is also actually encouraged and in many ways incorporated into the existing political structure.[1]

De Cocq draws a further contrast between American and European self-help groups:

A distinction can be made between the self-help group more or less homogeneous in its membership, which focuses on a single concern, and the heterogeneously composed self-help group, which may have many focuses of concern. The former concentrates on separate issues such as racial discrimination, housing, air pollution, urban transportation, poverty, and so on. Groups of this type seem more prevalent on the North American continent than in Western Europe.

In contrast, "multi-concern" or "multi-focus" self-help groups have broader social-philosophical goals, under which numerous issues can be subsumed. Such goals might include improving the quality of life or the humanization of a technocratically oriented society. Many self-help groups of this type are found in Europe.

De Cocq's observations emphasize that, as is the case in the United States, European self-help groups reflect the prevailing socioeconomic climates in their countries. What follows are brief sketches of how self-help groups and the national government policies pertaining to them have developed in Canada, western Germany, and Great Britain. Smaller European countries—Belgium and the Netherlands, for instance—have supported individual self-help groups when the government believed that the groups were helping sufferers of a problem for which no other services existed. This seems to be the accepted social policy in European countries that, in varying degrees, encompass "welfare-state" philosophy and programs.

**Canada** It is natural to start with the self-help scene in our near northern neighbor, Canada. Canadian self-help developments have frequently been linked with those in the United States because of the rapid increase in the range and number of groups, the creation of clearinghouses, a good deal of professional interest, and research done by academics and others. Geography and language have made possible a substantial interaction and mutual influence regarding self-help between the two countries, with exchange of materials, reciprocal attendance at meetings, consideration of common issues, and so forth.

Legislatively, however, Canadian authorities have been far more active than their U.S. counterparts. Canada's central government in Ottawa has shown a willingness to explore, support, and promote self-help-group activities that probably exceeds that of any other current government body. Self-help groups began to be prominent in Canada in the early or mid-1970s. By 1980 the Health Promotion Branch of Health and Welfare, Canada (the equivalent of the U.S. Department of Health and Human Services), began to conduct research seeking to document the country's self-help groups and to produce educational materials about self-help for the public and professionals. A bimonthly self-help newsletter in English and French has been published since 1982.

Two excellent hour-long documentary films have been produced and widely distributed: one is a general overview of the origins and functioning of self-help groups of both the 12-step and non-12-step variety and includes both Canadian and U.S. materials; the other details the functioning of a personal-exploration group and its effects on participants.

Additionally, the Health Promotion Branch has published books dealing with the role of self-help in chronic disease, how to organize a group, relationships with professionals, and other topics. The branch has sponsored, subsidized, and participated in a number of Canada-wide and regional or provincial conferences on self-help issues. In the fall of 1992 it sponsored an international self-help conference in Ottawa. Canadian professionals and academics have been influenced by these initiatives and—considering the vast population disparity between the two countries —have introduced courses, conducted self-help research, and consulted and written about the self-help phenomenon to a greater degree than have professionals in the United States.

The role of Canada's central government in self-help has been educational and promotive. It has not provided direct financial support for groups' operations, as have some European countries, and consequently the issues of government control and surveillance, of group accountability, have not been prominent in Canada. A lively controversy about the sponsorship, financing, and staffing of Canada's self-help clearinghouses has been sparked, however. The importance of clearinghouses to provide accurate information on existing groups and services, especially in large cities, and how they can be contacted is acknowledged and accepted by all. In Toronto and Montreal, however, self-help groups believe that they should organize and run the clearinghouses free of government and professional participation. The groups have wanted government to support clearinghouses financially but not to decide on their programs or staffs. This controversy has not been fully resolved, although some clearinghouses continue to receive revenues from government and private agencies.

**Germany**   In the former Federal Republic of Germany (now united with the former German Democratic Republic) the number of known self-help groups doubled between 1980 and 1984, from 30,000 to 60,000, showing an annual increase of 20 percent.[2] Despite this rapid growth, however, it was estimated that not more than 2.3 percent of the population over age 15 participated in them (Balke, 1989). This relatively limited public participation did not prevent a good deal of expressions of support by most German political parties for self-help ideals and activities. The verbal expressions were implemented by financial subsidies to self-help groups from local, regional, and state governments. Jürgen Matzat, an experienced observer of German self-help activities, wrote in 1987,

> In the Federal Republic of Germany today there is almost no politically relevant grouping which does not make an appropriate statement in its own programmes. Thus the politics of the self-help ideology have achieved a high status in public discussion—something which had before only to some extent been achieved by the patients' own organizations or by academic investigations.
>
> Of course, this state support tends to assist mostly self-help groups within the welfare system, to assist rather less self-help groups outside the welfare system, and to assist hardly at all those groups working against the welfare system.[3]

Arpad Barath has elaborated on the acceptance of self-help groups in Germany: "There came about an increasing recognition of self-help groups, first from local authorities, and later from higher-order institutions such as Government agencies, health authorities. Second, self-help gains an ever-widening public recognition and intellectual support from many community-action research projects initiated by insightful community leaders, devoted academicians, responsive politicians and the like."[4]

The financial support to local self-help groups by various branches and agencies of the German government totaled more than $2 million in 1986. This comparatively generous support—for both program operations and self-help research—has been questioned by German self-help organizations on two grounds: first, that it is selective, with certain self-help groups being excluded, and, second, that the money received may be corrupting and may distort or divert the original purposes of the groups receiving it.

The latter issue continues to be actively debated in Germany, and it also includes the fear that self-help is supported by government bodies because it is less expensive than professional service. Matzat discusses these points:

> The administration assesses and classifies self-help groups according to their "suitability for support." In this way, the critical cutting edge of the self-help movement is blunted. More and more this "alternative form of care" becomes self-care and hence care on the cheap. We are already seeing the emergence of initial plans for "comprehensive care" by self-help groups (for example in the cancer sphere), and there are lines of thinking which would "condemn" alcoholics to participate in self-help groups (for example to regain their driving license). One cannot overlook the danger of self-help groups being appropriated and instrumentalized by state planning. (1987, 43)

Germany has also seen widespread growth of self-help clearinghouses that aid and provide information about local self-help groups. At least 200 clearinghouses exist in Germany (as compared with about 45 in the United States), and the central German government partially funds a national federation of self-help clearinghouses based in Berlin, which organizes conferences, publishes literature, and negotiates with the central government, private philanthropies, and business groups.

**Great Britain**  Another populous country in which many self-help groups have arisen is Great Britain. It is estimated that more than 50,000 groups existed there in 1988, a rapid growth having occurred since 1979, when 10,000 groups were reported.[5] Responding to this growth, the government's Department of Health and Social Services (DHSS) in 1986 appropriated £1.6 million to support self-help activities.

Differing from the German pattern of direct subsidies to individual self-help groups, the British DHSS established 18 local support centers in major cities and involved in them established charitable organizations as well as area health authorities and social service departments. These bodies then determined which self-help groups should get funding. Self-help groups serving the elderly, disabled persons, the chronically ill and their families, and handicapped children were chosen as high priorities in most localities. The project was planned to run for three years as a demonstration experiment and was to be carefully evaluated by a well-known London research organization, the Tavistock Institute.

## Role of International Agencies

Discussion of governmental policies toward self-help would not be complete without describing the influence of some international agencies. Among United Nations–affiliated agencies, the World Health Organization (WHO) has been outstandingly active in promoting self-help approaches. Since 1980 its European regional office in Copenhagen has organized a dozen conferences on self-help and self-care, published materials in several languages, and set up a Europe-wide self-help clearinghouse in Belgium. These activities have undoubtedly had a positive influence on government attitudes and policies toward self-help in the countries discussed, and on others in the region. At a 1986 meeting in Canada the WHO adopted a document on health promotion that came to be known as the Ottawa Charter, which calls for specifically enhancing self-help and other forms of social support in the community.

## Some Alternate Possibilities

In Germany, where local-government subsidies to groups is an established policy, many self-help analysts and groups themselves are uneasy at what they perceive as the selective support given to those groups which do not threaten or challenge orthodox, established programs but are viewed as supplementing them or providing them more cheaply. Groups that do challenge or criticize established professional methods or political ideas are not supported, and this differential treatment is seen as an indirect way of controlling groups and in basic opposition to self-help philosophy. While compromises relating to this conflict can be found, they are usually local, short-lived, and do not reflect broad central-government policy.

Lacking such direct subsidies, many self-help groups in the United States have found it necessary to go in for large-scale fund-raising. This highly specialized activity developed in the United States and is aimed especially at corporations and wealthy individuals. It requires the hiring of professional fund-raisers and often involves the participation in group decision-making of persons not affected by the common problem. These factors, as noted in Chapter 6, can change the original character of self-help groups and lead to membership dissatisfaction.

One alternative to these problem-creating direct government subsidies to groups is Canada's policy that government should educate the public and professionals about self-help and promote the ideas of self-help organizations, in the belief that financial backing from corporations and the public will then be more easily attained.

Another policy alternative—and one being explored in the United States—is for private insurance companies to pay service fees to groups when an insured member is assisted, in the same way that fees for medical or psychiatric care are paid to individual professionals and agencies. Such a system would be complicated and slow to develop, but in principle it seems a reasonable idea and would of course provide a measure of financial help to some self-help groups and would entail no government intervention and surveillance. Such payments to self-help groups for services rendered to individuals could be made no matter who the insurer—private corporations or the government itself if some form of national health insurance were adopted. Some eligibility criteria would be necessary for insurance payments—probably having to do with a group's size, stability, length of existence, staffing, and so forth—but self-help groups would probably accept such criteria as less restrictive and controlling than government supervision.

Of these alternatives, the Canadian government policy of education about and promotion of self-help groups without subsidizing them seems to be the most practical and least problematic. The natural question arises of how translatable the model is. Did it evolve from sociopolitical factors peculiar to Canada or was it fortuitously arrived at by imaginative government functionaries there, who had an intimate understanding of self-help ideas and consciously avoided a fiscal relationship that would involve supervision and surveillance? Not enough is known about the policy's origins to discuss the latter question, and, as each country's sociopolitical climate is distinctive, little can be stated about the potential translatability of the Canadian model. What is essential, however, is opportunities for dialogue among the groups themselves and between them, government functionaries, and influential political forces outside of government—a process that could go on for a long time. Basic government recognition and acknowledgment of self-help-group contributions in the United States took some 25 years to achieve, and effecting a workable arrangement that includes some mutually acceptable pattern of financing would probably require a comparable period of time.

As some groups serving health and mental-health needs continue their campaign to receive payments from insurance carriers for services rendered, we can expect some initial breakthroughs toward this alternative in a lesser time—perhaps 10 years. Self-help analysts Marion Jacobs and Gerald Goodman have advanced the idea that in coming years private health-care organizations such as health maintenance organizations (HMOs) will create and extensively use self-help groups for the patients they serve.[6] There does not seem to be any credible evidence at present to support this contention, however desirable it might be, and as the private health-care industry is profit-oriented and highly competitive, such a development seems unlikely.

The greater probability is that established self-help groups and clearinghouses in the United States will continue to struggle financially; some will be successful in fund-raising and endure, others will not. In this connection, it is worth noting that many 12-step groups seem to be more durable than some of the non-12-step ones. The explanation for this difference seems to lie both in the numbers of actual and potential members who suffer from a chemical or psychological addiction and in the conscious minimization by 12-step groups of staff and bureaucratic arrangements and of some forms of centralized control. Since one of the tenets of 12-step groups is to avoid taking political positions, they might see acceptance of any form of government subsidies as incompatible with 12-step philosophy. Also, 12-step groups generally have not gone in for public fund-raising campaigns. None of these limitations, however, seem to have impaired their growth and appeal, since they continue to be one of the most rapidly expanding sectors of self-help.

*Chapter 10*

# Self-Help as a Social Movement

Throughout this book much material has been presented on self-help groups as a general phenomenon. The many topics discussed include the organization and functioning characteristics of 12-step and non-12-step groups: members' motivations for joining and their perceptions of groups; the activities groups engage in; and self-help group relationships with private and public human-services programs and professionals.

In this concluding chapter I address the very important question of whether, in view of the great diversity among self-help groups, they can be regarded as a unified social movement. In doing so I also take into account some recent developments and trends that are crucial to forming such a judgment.

## Characteristics of a Social Movement

We are accustomed to thinking of social movements as built around single issues—for instance, opposing the Vietnam War or legal abortion or, as with the women's and environmental movements, dealing with a host of related issues from a consistent viewpoint. Social movements generally arise when individuals act collectively, agreeing on a goal and an ideology. Strategies and tactics usually develop to influence policy and to bring about desired sociopolitical changes.

Most definitions and analyses of social movements emphasize their common purposes and ideas and their objective of effecting social change. "The essence of a social movement is change," writes William Cameron, adding that "the main characteristic of a social movement is that it seeks to change the culture or change the social structure or redistribute the power of control within a society."[1] Ralph Turner and Lewis Killian speak of a social movement as "a collectivity acting with some continuity to promote change in the society or group to which it is a part."[2] Their definition adds the element of *continuity* or duration to the possession of an ideology and a sense of common purpose. A social movement's further requisite is a structure or organization to recruit and hold a membership and to administer to the common actions to secure the agreed-upon goal.

Very broadly, self-help groups have influentially shaped public attitudes and policies regarding the values of mutual aid, social support, and taking personal responsibility for change through participation in non-bureaucratic small groups. Even though self-help organizations lack a single common goal, a definable constituency, and a unified organizational structure, their substantial efforts to raise public consciousness and affect policy are immeasurable but incontestable.

Additionally, it is important to understand how a social movement serves both its followers and the whole society. For it acts as a kind of social cement that binds people into a "we-group" from which they draw support and identity. For the wider society it often educates the public about—and may thereby popularize—previously unacceptable ideas, policies, and practices. This wider acceptance and integration into the cultural mainstream of opinions formerly considered deviant is experienced positively by the movement's supporters, who may sense a reduction in their personal anomie and isolation.

Thus what distinguish the usual kind of social movement from other collective phenomena are (a) an ideology, (b) a sense of common purpose or "we-ness," (c) a structure, and (d) an action plan: development of strategy and tactics.

## Self-Help Groups and Social Movement Criteria

**Ideology** There seems to be no question that all self-help groups reflect ideas and views that are especially appealing and relevant to their members. The ideas may be conscious, explicit, well-formulated, and tested over time, as in 12-step groups like A.A. But they can also be implicit, not necessarily conscious and not systematically formulated, as in the case of many non-12-step groups, especially new, small, and unaffiliated ones.

One successful non-12-step group with a large membership, chapters in many places, and a long history but apparently no specific ideology is Parents without Partners. This organization was analyzed in *The Strength in US* (1976) as follows:

> In contrast to personal growth groups, PWP does not seem to carry out searching and meaningful group discussions of the problems many members have in common as single parents. The "consciousness-raising" techniques of the Women's Movement would seem to be ideally adapted to the needs of PWP members, since the basis of that method is to help members realize the relationship of personal to social problems, define and deal with their feelings about men, their sexuality, the institution of marriage, sex discrimination, and related topics. PWP has not seemed to want to travel that path, which could lead to the questioning of many basic social values. Indeed, the very name Parents WITHOUT Partners seems to imply an initial acceptance of the stigma of an inferior position; the belief is that "parents WITH partners"—in keeping with the prevailing social norm—are better. (Katz and Bender 1976, 69)

One can discern in many health-oriented self-help groups that do not articulate a conscious, explicit ideology or an underlying formal belief system a popularly held network of ideas that serve to attract members. These may include skepticism about conventional medical care, health professionals, and the treatments these professionals prescribe; belief in self-care, self-regulation, and the importance of morale in overcoming a physical problem; conviction that the problem was caused by external factors, not by the individual's behavior. One or more of these ideas may motivate new members, who absorb others of them through their participation in the group. For cancer patients, for example, group optimism about patients' outcome is often a part of the group's belief system. In all the chronic disease groups, the ideology, whether explicit or unstated, emphasizes the patient's ability to better adjust to the social problems the disease entails and thus to influence life-style changes that will allow him or her to better cope with the problems of daily life.

**"We-ness"** The feeling of "we-ness"—of being part of a group that shares and does something about a common problem—is a basic binding force in self-help groups. A collective identification with and loyalty to the group develops, regardless of whether the group's antagonists are perceived as external—professionals, the "system," government policies, indifference or lack of understanding by the public—or internal—the problem-creating and -perpetuating behavior that arises from psychological or other factors specific to the member. "We-ness" feelings are mobilized in the classic model of social movements—sometimes referred to as "instrumental"—by having an external antagonist or barrier, such as "mainstream" social attitudes and/or policies. But in 12-step groups, which eschew social action to change policies, "we-ness" feelings develop strongly from the sense of being in the same boat and confronting the common enemy of self-destructive internal beliefs and behavior. Collective feelings of this kind, which are potent in binding members to the self-help group, reflect and relate to the group's ideology, whether explicit or implicit.

**Structure and Organization**  To remain functional, to attract new members, and to work toward the common goals, every self-help group needs at least an elementary organizational structure, which usually involves some division of labor and sharing of responsibilities. Sometimes the structure is preset, as happens when a local unit of a national self-help organization such as Recovery, Inc. is established: the ground rules, officers, committees, and meeting procedures already exist. New ad hoc or unaffiliated groups develop their own structures and organizational arrangements, often through trial and error. Some groups choose to remain small, local, and unaffiliated; others seek to grow, proselytize, and expand to the variety of activities that are found among the many self-help groups that endure and become influential, and come to be recognized as important resources in meeting a problem. Some writers refer to the latter type as "self-help organizations" and the former as "self-help groups." The considerations for making this distinction are not clear, but differences of scale and scope of activities may affect whether or not the criteria for a social movement are present.

**Action Plan**  Closely related to ideology and structure is the group's plan of action, what kinds of things it sees itself doing in working toward its goals. In the case of 12-step groups, these are mainly personal change for members, with the assumption that as the 12-step methodology becomes recognized as effective, more and more people who have unsuccessfully coped with the problem or addiction will be drawn into an existing unit or form a new group that follows 12-step organizational principles and methodologies.

Many non-12-step groups experience a steady expansion of activities, often adding elements that may not have been contemplated by the original founders. Some activities—having outside speakers, publishing newsletters and other literature, arranging for resources to meet member needs, such as transportation, child or respite care—are designed to help members; some are aimed at influencing professionals and agencies in the community; others seek to educate the public and influential figures in the community about the problem. Disagreements about tactics and strategies and consequent schisms, breakaways, and dissolution may arise in all forms of self-help groups, as they do in other social movements.

## Are Self-Help Groups a Movement?

Given that to varying degrees self-help groups and organizations embody the characteristics that define a social movement, can it then be concluded that the world of self-help constitutes a social movement, perhaps of a special kind?

Because of their huge diversity, it would seem more accurate on the whole to refer to self-help manifestations as a social *trend* rather than a social movement. In some ways, all the varied self-help phenomena analyzed resemble how Patricia Barry et al. have described the closely related field of self-care in health:

> The self-care movement is more a collection of programs and activities than it is a concerted political force. Self-care is not part of a broader, identified, political movement; there is no large constituency engaged in an effort to reduce utilization, reduce costs, or make the practice of medicine more humane. Such a concerted effort demands well-articulated goals, consolidated support, and committed leadership. *The self-care movement does not seem to have any of these requirements.*[3]

Similarly, self-help is not, at least at present, a concerted political force, identified as such, with specific aims, programs, a constituency, and a recognized leadership. It is a congeries of diverse programs and activities, sharing some general ideological principles but having an enormous variety of specifics.

One way of considering self-help groups as a social movement, however, is to keep in mind the very significant differences between 12-step and non-12-step groups that have constituted a major theme and analytical premise in this book. Much more so than with any other collection of self-help groups that focus on different problems, the large and growing collectivity of 12-step groups should thus probably be thought of as constituting a social movement of a special kind.

**"Expressive" Movements and 12-Step Groups**　Herbert Blumer, a leading theorist of social movements, has described an "expressive" category of them, in contrast to the classic model or "instrumental" type outlined and discussed earlier in this chapter. Blumer writes, "The characteristic feature of expressive movements is that they do not seek to change the institutions of the social order. . . . [T]he tension and unrest out of which they emerge are not focussed upon some objective of social change. . . . Instead, they are released in some type of expressive behavior, which, however, in becoming crystallized, may have profound effects on the personalities of individuals."[4] Blumer's concept of an "expressive" type of social movement has not been developed further or applied by other writers on self-help, but it substantially supports the case for looking on 12-step groups as constituting a special kind of social movement.

Using the categorical distinction "expressive," we might say that *some* 12-step groups meet the classic model criteria and thus constitute social movements in their own right. For example, A.A. certainly qualifies to be called a social movement by reason of its history, duration, and steady growth, its wide public influence in changing concepts of alcoholism, and its ability to retain the adherence and participation of many members. While not having all these elements, non-12-step organizations such as self-help groups of disabled persons and of the elderly also seem to meet the classic social movement criteria.

Under the broad framework of a major social trend, which encompasses a variety of self-help-group programs and ideas, there are thus found some social movements organized by special populations to accomplish specific goals.

**Coalitions**　Another tendency of social movements that needs discussion are initiatives undertaken to bring about a greater degree of cooperation and coalition among separate self-help organizations. Recent examples are the Alliance of Genetic Support Groups—a coalition of some 150 national and local self-help organizations in fields such as hemophilia, sickle-cell disease, and cystic fibrosis—and the National Organization for Rare Disorders (NORD)—a coalition for sufferers of "orphan" diseases.

The groups that participate in the Genetic Alliance remain autonomous, but the liaison body performs some social movement functions, considered from the viewpoint of the cooperating groups. The alliance seeks to upgrade public and professional understanding, research, and government support for sufferers or potential sufferers:

> The Alliance is dedicated to fostering a strong partnership among consumers and professionals to enhance education and service for families with genetic disorders and to represent their needs. Its board of directors, composed of consumers and health professionals, seeks to increase awareness about genetic disorders by developing and distributing materials for the public and for professionals, encourages communication among support groups, and promotes awareness of cross-disability similarities and resources. The Alliance is trying to improve the availability and appropriateness of genetic services by identifying gaps in services to individuals in its member organizations and by developing model programs or recommendations to fill those gaps. It also has sought to identify the health-care financing needs of these people.[5]

The ideology thus stresses comprehensive professional and government service programs in a relatively neglected field and more money for research and professional education. It has an organizational structure for facilitating its work; it engages in lobbying and other actions. Most members of the affiliated genetic disease self-help groups, however, are probably interested mainly in remedial actions for their particular problem and do not identify with the alliance's broader social-movement objectives.

Founded in 1986, NORD is an educational, coordinating, and lobbying body for the estimated 2,000 rare or "orphan" diseases that have a relatively small number of sufferers in the United States. By NORD's definition a "rare" disease has fewer than 200,000 sufferers—thought to be too small a potential market to warrant research and development efforts by pharmaceutical companies. NORD's social-movement functions are spelled out in the following statements from its official document:

> To act as a clearinghouse for information about rare disorders and to network families with similar disorders together for mutual support.
> To foster communication among rare disease voluntary agencies, government bodies, industry, scientific researchers, academic institutions and concerned individuals.
> To encourage and promote increased scientific research on the cause, control and ultimate cure of rare disorders.

To accumulate and disseminate information about Orphan Drugs and Devices, making known their availability to patients, physicians and other concerned parties.

To assist in harmonizing and making more efficient the work of voluntary agencies and to offer technical assistance to newly organized support groups.

To educate the general public and medical profession about the existence, diagnosis and treatment of rare disorders.

To represent people with Orphan Diseases who are not otherwise represented by organizations or voluntary agencies.

To focus the attention of government, industry and the scientific community on the needs of people with rare disorders.[6]

As these two examples show, it is easier to form coalitions of groups in a closely related field, such as a particular kind of health problem—genetic or rare diseases—than more generally in problem-unrelated self-help groups.

Despite their similarities in ideology, structure, and methodology, the 150 to 200 independent 12-step groups in the United States have not found it necessary to set up a liaison or coordinating supraorganization. This is probably because most of them have closely copied the A.A. model and experience. In fact, most new 12-step groups seek the approval of A.A.; since A.A.'s founding in 1935, "148 groups, each with a different problem focus, have requested permission to use the 12 Steps. Most of these requests occurred from 1985 to 1990."[7] As this statement suggests, 12-step groups showed a phenomenal growth, particularly in the 1980s, and have captured much recent attention.

An important recent development with bearing on the social movement aspects of self-help groups is the creation of some national coordinating structures to monitor and help implement the recommendations of Surgeon-General C. Everett Koop's September 1987 Workshop on Self-Help and Public Health, which marked recognition and support of the role of self-help activities in health.

The dimension of seeking to bring about social change—in beliefs, attitudes, and formalized policies—certainly constitutes one of the important defining criteria for an "instrumental" social movement. While at present more of a "trend" than a "movement," self-help's social role has been and continues to be constant, dynamic, and extremely flexible. Its full potential as an innovative social form has hardly begun to be realized, but it is increasingly taking on social movement characteristics and functions.

# *Appendix*

## Classification of Self-Help Groups by Primary Focus

<u>Type 1: Therapeutic</u>

A  Mental-health organizations (overcoming specific psychological problems). Examples: Recovery, Inc., National Alliance for the Mentally Ill, GROW, Neurotics Anonymous, Emotions Anonymous
B  Addiction organizations. Examples: Alcoholics Anonymous, Al-Anon, Alateen, Narcotics Anonymous, Overeaters Anonymous
C  Physical-health organizations
   1  Disease-specific. Examples: Make Today Count, Mended Hearts, Lost Chord Club, renal dialysis groups
   2  Family-oriented. Examples: Parents of Children with Learning Disabilities, Candlelighters, SIDS, Friends and Family of Schizophrenics
   3  Multidiagnostic. Example: Centers for Independent Living
D  Life-transition organizations. Examples: widow/widower groups, Alone Again, Alone Together, retiree groups, divorce groups
E  Stress-reduction organizations. Example: Santa Monica Peer-Counseling Center

<u>Type 2: Social Advocacy/Action</u>

A  Organizations created to overcome a single problem. Examples: Mothers against Drunk Driving, welfare-rights organizations, Coalition for the Rights of the Disabled
B  Organizations created on the basis of age. Example: Gray Panthers
C  Organizations created to further ethnic minorities. Examples: Alianza Hispano-Americana, Black Single Mothers Association

Type 3: Groups Created to Support Alternative Life-styles

A  Gay-liberation organizations
B  Urban and rural residential communes

Type 4: Groups Providing Havens via a 24-Hour Live-in Situation

Examples: Daytop Village, Delancey Street, shelters for battered women

Type 5: Mixed Types (More than One Primary Focus)

A  Ex-prisoner associations. Examples: Fortune Society, Seventh Step Foundation
B  Social-therapeutic/family-oriented groups. Examples: Parents without Partners, Families Anonymous
C  Economic
   1  Food banks
   2  Housing organizations
   3  Consumer/producer cooperatives. Examples: Amish, Doukhobours, Hutterites
   4  Other economic. Examples: 40+ Club, Debtors Anonymous, Checks Anonymous

---

From Alfred H. Katz and Eugene I. Bender, *Helping One Another: Self-Help Groups in a Changing World* (Oakland, Calif.: Third Party Publishers, 1990), 27.

# Notes

## 1. Introduction

1. Alfred H. Katz and Eugene I. Bender, *The Strength in US: Self-Help Groups in the Modern World* (New York: New Viewpoints, 1976), 36; hereafter cited in text.

2. *The Voluntary Sector* (New York: Academy for Educational Development, 1980).

3. U.S. Department of Health and Human Services, *Health in the 1990s* (Washington, D.C.: U.S. Government Printing Office, 1983), 33.

4. Gerald Leventhal, Kenneth Maton, Edward Madara, and Marisa Julien, "The Birth and Death of Self-Help Groups: An Ecological Perspective," in *Helping One Another: Self-Help Groups in a Changing World*, ed. Alfred H. Katz and Eugene I. Bender (Oakland, Calif.: Third Party Publishers, 1990), 105–22.

5. Peter Kropotkin, *Mutual Aid: A Factor in Evolution* (London: Penguin Books, 1939), 234 (my italics).

6. Edward Thompson, *The Making of the English Working Class* (London: Victor Gollancz, 1963), 200.

7. Beatrice Webb, *The Cooperative Movement in Great Britain*, 2d ed. (London: Swain Sonnenschein, 1893), 41.

8. John R. Commons, *History of Labor in the United States* (New York: Macmillan, 1961).

9. Oscar Handlin, ed., *Immigration as a Factor in American History* (Englewood Cliffs, N.J.: Prentice-Hall, 1959).

## 2. The Two Primary Types of Self-Help Groups

1. *Self-Help Sourcebook* (Denville, N.J.: Self-Help Clearinghouse, 1988).

113

2. Elizabeth Ogg, "Partners in Coping," Public Affairs Pamphlet no. 559 (New York: Public Affairs Committee, 1978), 1; hereafter cited in text.

3. *Alcoholics Anonymous*, 3d ed. (New York: A.A. World Services, 1976), 59–60; hereafter cited in text as *AA*.

4. Christina C. Fox, statement prepared for the conference Self-Help Groups, Life-Threatening Illness, and Grief, New Jersey Self-Help Clearinghouse, Denville, N.J., January 1990.

5. Lee Miller, statement prepared for the conference Self-Help Groups, Life-Threatening Illness, and Grief.

6. Catherine Logan, statement prepared for the conference Self-Help Groups, Life-Threatening Illness, and Grief.

7. Marcia Alig, statement prepared for the conference Self-Help Groups, Life-Threatening Illness, and Grief.

8. Denise Furster, statement prepared for the conference Self-Help Groups, Life-Threatening Illness, and Grief.

## *3. Common Characteristics of Self-Help Groups*

1. Leon Levy, "Self-Help Groups: Types and Psychological Processes," *Journal of Behavioral Science* 12 (September 1976): 314–15; hereafter cited in text.

2. British National Council of Single Parents (London) newsletter, no. 4, April 1981, 3.

3. Agnes Hatfield, "Self-Help Groups for Families of the Mentally Ill," *Social Work* 26 (1981): 412; hereafter cited in text.

4. Phyllis Silverman and Diane Smith, "Helping in Mutual Help Groups for the Physically Diasbled," in *The Self-Help Revolution*, ed. Alan Gartner and Frank Riessman (New York: Human Sciences Press, 1984), 86; hereafter cited in text.

5. Alfred H. Katz, *Hemophilia: A Study in Hope and Reality* (Springfield, Ill.: Charles C. Thomas, 1970).

6. Margaret Yoak and Mark Chesler, "Alternative Professional Roles in Health Care Delivery: Leadership Patterns in Self-Help Groups," *Journal of Applied Behavioral Science* 21, no. 4 (1985): 438.

7. Bob Knight, Richard Wollert, Leon Levy, Cynthia Frame, and Valerie Padget, "Self-Help Groups: The Members' Perspective," *American Journal of Community Psychology* 8 (1980): 61.

8. Richard Wollert, Leon Levy, and Bob Knight, "Help-Giving in Behavioral Control and Stress-Coping Self-Help Groups," *Small Group Behavior* 13 (1982): 37–38.

9. John Eccles, "A Group for Mothers of the Mentally Retarded," *Australian Mental Retardation Digest* 12 (1981): 17.

10. David Robinson, "The Self-Help Component of Primary Health Care," *Social Science and Medicine* 14a (January 1980): 418.

11. "Self-Concept," in *International Encyclopedia of Psychiatry, Psychology, Psychoanalysis and Neurology,* vol. 10, ed. Bernard Wolman (New York: Aesculapius, 1977), 115.

12. Albert Bandura, *Social Learning Theory* (Englewood Cliffs, N.J.: Prentice-Hall, 1977).

## 4. What Makes Self-Help Groups Work?

1. Abraham Maslow, *Motivation and Personality,* 2d ed. (New York: Harper & Row, 1970).

2. Marshall Clinard, *The Sociology of Deviant Behavior* (New York: Holt, Rinehart & Winston, 1974), 23.

3. Alfred H. Katz, "Self-Help Organizations and Volunteer Participation in Social Welfare," *Social Work* 15, no. 1 (1970).

4. Miriam Stewart, "Expanding Theoretical Conceptualizations of Self-Help Groups," *Social Science and Medicine* 21, no. 9 (1990).

5. Albert Bandura, "Model of Causality in Social Learning Theory," in *Cognition and Psychotherapy,* ed. Michael Mahoney and Arthur Freeman (New York: Plenum, 1985), 88–89; hereafter cited in text.

6. Albert Bandura, *Social Foundations of Thought and Action: A Social Cognitive Theory* (Englewood Cliffs, N.J.: Prentice-Hall, 1986), 347.

7. Albert Bandura, "Toward a Unifying Theory of Behavioral Change," *Psychological Review* 84, no. 2 (1977): 197.

8. Lisa Berkman and Leonard Syme, "Social Networks, Host Resistance, and Mortality: A Nine-Year Follow-up Study of Alameda County Residents," *American Journal of Epidemiology* 109, no. 2 (1978): 190–92.

9. Marc Pilisuk, "Delivery of Social Support: The Social Inoculation," *American Journal of Orthopsychiatry* 52, no. 1 (1982): 24.

10. Jan Palmblad, "Stress and Immunological Competence: Studies in Man," in *Psychoneuroimmunology,* ed. Robert Ader (New York: Academic Press, 1981), 229–57.

11. Marc Pilisuk and Susan Parks, *The Healing Web: Social Networks and Human Survival* (Hanover, N.H.: University Press of New England, 1986), 42; hereafter cited in text.

12. Robert Ader, preface to *Psychoneuroimmunology,* xiii.

## 5. Case Studies of Two Successful Groups

1. Harriet Shelter, *A History of the National Alliance for the Mentally Ill* (Arlington, Va.: National Alliance for the Mentally Ill, 1986), 2–4; hereafter cited in text as *NAMI.*

2. Agnes Hatfield, "The National Alliance for the Mentally Ill: A Decade Later," *Community Mental Health Journal* 27, no. 2 (1991): 100.

3. Timmen Cermak, Terry Hunt, Bonnie Keene, and Thomas W., "Co-dependency: More than a Catchword," *Patient Care*, 15 August 1989, 132; hereafter cited in text.

4. Timmen Cermak, "Diagnostic Criteria for Co-dependency," *Journal of Psychoactive Drugs* 18 (1986): 15–20.

5. ACA Interview, pamphlet (Torrance, Calif.: World Service Organization, 1990).

6. Rhonda Elwell, "Adult Children of Alcoholics," unpublished manuscript.

7. *The Problem and the Solution* (Van Nuys, Calif.: Adult Children of Alcoholics, 1987).

## 6. Leadership, Growth Patterns, and the Role of Ideology

1. Alfred H. Katz, *Parents of the Handicapped* (Springfield, Ill.: Charles C. Thomas, 1961), 111, 114.

2. *Alcoholics Anonymous*, 2d ed. (New York: A.A. World Services, 1961), 567.

3. *A.A. Comes of Age* (New York: A.A. World Services, 1957), 112.

4. Hazel Johnson, "Alcoholics Anonymous in the 1980s: Variations on a Theme," unpublished paper, 1986; hereafter cited in text.

5. Kenneth Maton, Gerald Leventhal, Edward Madara, and Marisa Julien, "The Birth and Death of Self-Help Groups: A Population Ecology Perspective," in Katz and Bender, *Helping One Another*, 105–22.

6. Stephanie Riger, "Vehicles for Empowerment: The Case of Feminist Movement Organizations," *Prevention in Human Services* 3 (1983–84): 99–111.

## 7. Relations between Self-Help Groups and Professionals

1. Peter Abrams, "Social Change, Social Networks, and Neighborhood Care," *Social Work Service*, no. 22 (1980): 16.

2. Olive Stevenson, *Specialization in Social Service Teams* (London: Allen & Unwin, 1981); Roy Pinker, "An Alternative View," in *Social Workers: Their Role and Tasks* (London: Bedford Square Press, 1982), 232–62.

3. Morton Lieberman and Leonard Borman, *Self-Help Groups for Coping with Crisis* (San Francisco: Jossey-Fass, 1979), 28–37.

4. Jean-Marie Romeder, *Self-Help Groups in Canada* (Ottawa: Health and Welfare Canada, 1982), 13.

5. Zachary Gussow and George Tracy, "Self-Help Health Groups: A Grass Roots Response to a Need for Services," *Journal of Applied Behavioral Science* 12 (September 1976): 390.

6. Ronald Toseland and Lynda Hacker, "Self-Help Groups and Professional Involvement," *Social Work* 27 (July 1982): 341–47.

7. Edward Madara and Camille Grish, "Finding Out More about How Self-Help Groups Help," *Network*, August–September 1981, 3.

8. Robert Emerick, "Self-Help Groups for Former Patients: Relations with Mental Health Professionals," *Hospital and Community Psychiatry* 41 (April 1990): 401–2; hereafter cited in text.

9. Rita Black and Diane Drachman, "Hospital Social Workers and Self-Help Groups," *Health and Social Work* 10 (Spring 1985): 99.

10. Nancy Bryant, "Self-Help Groups and Professionals—Cooperation or Conflict?," in Katz and Bender, *Helping One Another*, 183–95.

11. Leon Levy, "Self-Help Groups Viewed by Mental Health Professionals," *American Journal of Community Psychology* 6 (August 1978): 305–13.

12. Linda Kurtz, "Cooperation and Rivalry between Helping Professionals and Members of A.A.," *Health and Social Work* 10 (Spring 1985): 104–12.

13. Alan Gartner and Frank Riessman, "Made for Each Other: Self-Help Groups and Mental Health Agencies," *Community Mental Health* 13 (1980): 28–32; hereafter cited in text.

14. C. Everett Koop, *Proceedings, Surgeon-General's Workshop on Self-Help and Public Health* (Washington, D.C.: U.S. Department of Health and Human Services, 1988), 13.

15. In 1979 Jared Hermalin et al. studied 74 community mental-health centers, including social workers, nurses, and psychologists, who could name only one self-help group ("Enhancing Primary Prevention: The Marriage of Self-Help Groups and Formal Health Care Delivery Systems," *Journal of Clinical Child Psychology* 8, no. 2 [1979]: 125–29). Diane Zarem in 1982 sampled professionals in social work and psychology and found that they could name an average of three to four self-help groups ("Professional Involvement with Self-Help Groups," Ph.D. diss., University of California School of Social Welfare, Los Angeles). In contrast, Mary Bryant found in 1988 that more than 70 percent of nurses and social workers in San Diego public and private hospitals were familiar with and made referrals to eight to 12 self-help groups in the community ("Self-Help Groups and Professionals," in Katz and Bender, *Helping One Another*, 183–95).

16. *Psychology Today*, January 1988, 67.

17. *NASW News* [National Association of Social Workers, Silver Spring, Md.] 28, no. 2 (1983): 5.

18. Alfred H. Katz, "Self-Help Groups and Professionals: General Issues," in *Self-Help: Concepts and Applications*, ed. Alfred H. Katz et al. (Philadelphia: Charles Press, 1991), 59.

## 8. Populism and Social Action in Self-Help Groups

1. Regina Morantz, "19th-Century Health Reform and Women: A Program of Self-Help," in *Medicine without Doctors*, ed. Günter Risse, Ronald Numbers, and

Judith Leavitt (New York: Science History Publications, 1977), 78–81; hereafter cited in text.

2. Lawrence Goodwyn, "Populism and Powerlessness," in *The New Populism*, ed. Harry Boyte and Frank Riessman (Philadelphia: Temple University Press, 1986), 28; hereafter cited in text.

3. Cornel West, "Populism and Equality," in Boyte and Riessman, *The New Populism*, 208.

4. Robert Fisher, *Let the People Decide: Neighborhood Organizing in America* (Boston: Twayne Publishers, 1984), 111–14; hereafter cited in text.

5. Fitzhugh Mullan, "Self-Help Groups and Public Health," paper delivered at the symposium Self-Help and the Impact of Life-Threatening Conditions, Chicago, 1989.

6. National Marfan Foundation, *Connective Issues* 9, no. 2 (June 1990): 1.

## 9. Self-Help Groups and Public Policy

1. Gustave De Cocq, "European and North American Self-Help Movements: Some Contrasts," in Katz and Bender *Helping One Another*, 199; hereafter cited in text.

2. Klaus Balke, "Self-Help Groups and Social Policies: A Report about the Situation in West Germany," 1989, unpublished manuscript; hereafter cited in text.

3. Jürgen Matzat, "Self-Help Groups in West Germany," *Acta Psychiatrica Scandinavia* 76 (1987): 47; hereafter cited in text.

4. Arpad Barath, "Self-Help in Europe during the 1980s: A Critical Reading," 1991, unpublished manuscript.

5. Jan Branckaerts, *Summary of Self-Help in Europe* (Louvain, Belgium: World Health Organization International Self-Help Clearinghouse, 1990).

6. Marion Jacobs and Gerald Goodman, "Psychology and Self-Help Groups: Predictions on a Partnership," *American Psychologist*, January 1989, 1–10.

## 10. Self-Help as a Social Movement

1. William Cameron, *Modern Social Movements: A Sociological Outline* (New York: Random House, 1966), 8.

2. Ralph Turner and Lewis Killian, *Collective Behavior* (Englewood Cliffs, N.J.: Prentice-Hall, 1957), 13.

3. Patricia Barry et al., *Self-Care Programs* (Chapel Hill: University of North Carolina Health Services Research Center, 1979), 32.

4. Herbert Blumer, "Social Movements," in *Studies in Social Movements*, ed. B. McLaughlin (New York: Free Press, 1969), 23.

5. Joan Weiss, "Genetic Support Groups: A Continuum of Genetic Services," *Women and Health* 15, no. 3 (1989): 50–51.

6. Brochure of the National Organization for Rare Disorders, New Fairfield, Conn., 1989.

7. Melody Beattie, *Codependents' Guide to the 12 Steps* (Englewood Cliffs, N.J.: Prentice-Hall, 1987), 97.

# Bibliography

## Books

*A.A. Comes of Age*. New York: A.A. World Services, 1957.

Ader, Robert, ed. *Psychoneuroimmunology*. New York: Academic Press, 1981.

*Alcoholics Anonymous*, 2d ed. New York: A.A. World Services, 1961.

*Alcoholics Anonymous*, 3d ed. New York: A.A. World Services, 1976.

Bandura, Albert. *Social Foundations of Thought and Action: A Social Cognitive Theory*. Englewood Cliffs, N.J.: Prentice-Hall, 1986.

_____. *Social Learning Theory*. Englewood Cliffs, N.J.: Prentice-Hall, 1977.

Barry, Patricia, et al. *Self-Care Programs*. Chapel Hill: University of North Carolina Health Services Research Center, 1979.

Beattie, Melody. *Codependents' Guide to the 12 Steps*. Englewood Cliffs, N.J.: Prentice-Hall, 1987.

Branckaerts, Jan. *Summary of Self-Help in Europe*. Louvain, Belgium: World Health Organization International Self-Help Clearinghouse, 1990.

Cameron, William. *Modern Social Movements: A Sociological Outline*. New York: Random House, 1966.

Clinard, Marshall. *The Sociology of Deviant Behavior*. New York: Holt, Rinehart & Winston, 1974.

Gartner, Alan, and Frank Riessman, eds. *The Self-Help Revolution*. New York: Human Sciences Press, 1984.

Katz, Alfred H. *Hemophilia: A Study in Hope and Reality*. Springfield, Ill.: Charles C. Thomas, 1970.

_____. *Parents of the Handicapped*. Springfield, Ill.: Charles C. Thomas, 1961.

Katz, Alfred H., and Eugene I. Bender. *The Strength in US: Self-Help Groups in the Modern World*. New York: New Viewpoints, 1976.

Katz, Alfred H., and Eugene I. Bender, eds. *Helping One Another: Self-Help Groups in a Changing World.* Oakland, Calif.: Third Party Publishers, 1990.

Lieberman, Morton, and Leonard Borman. *Self-Help Groups for Coping with Crisis.* San Francisco: Jossey-Fass, 1979.

Maslow, Abraham. *Motivation and Personality.* 2d ed. New York: Harper & Row, 1970.

Pilisuk, Marc, and Susan Parks. *The Healing Web: Social Networks and Human Survival.* Hanover, N.H.: University Press of New England, 1986.

*The Problem and the Solution.* Van Nuys, Calif.: Adult Children of Alcoholics, 1987.

Romeder, Jean-Marie. *Self-Help Groups in Canada.* Ottawa: Health and Welfare Canada, 1982.

*Self-Help Sourcebook.* Denville, N.J.: Self-Help Clearinghouse, 1988.

Shelter, Harriet. *A History of the National Alliance for the Mentally Ill.* Arlington, Va.: National Alliance for the Mentally Ill, 1986.

Stevenson, Olive. *Specialization in Social Service Teams.* London: Allen & Unwin, 1981.

Turner, Ralph, and Lewis Killian. *Collective Behavior.* Englewood Cliffs, N.J.: Prentice-Hall, 1957.

U.S. Department of Health and Human Services. *Health in the 1990s.* Washington, D.C.: U.S. Government Printing Office, 1983.

_____. *Proceedings, Surgeon-General's Workshop on Self-Help and Public Health.* Washington, D.C.: U.S. Government Printing Office, 1988.

*The Voluntary Sector.* New York: Academy for Educational Development, 1980.

## Articles and Parts of Books

Abrams, Peter. "Social Change, Social Networks, and Neighborhood Care." *Social Work Service*, no. 22 (1980).

Bandura, Albert. "Model of Causality in Social Learning Theory." In *Cognition and Psychotherapy*, edited by Michael Mahoney and Arthur Freeman. New York: Plenum, 1985.

_____. "Toward a Unifying Theory of Behavioral Change." *Psychological Review* 84, no. 2 (1977).

Berkman, Lisa, and Leonard Syme. "Social Networks, Host Resistance, and Mortality: A Nine-Year Follow-up Study of Alameda County Residents." *American Journal of Epidemiology* 109, no. 2 (1978).

Black, Rita, and Diane Drachman. "Hospital Social Workers and Self-Help Groups." *Health and Social Work* 10 (Spring 1985).

Blumer, Herbert. "Social Movements." In *Studies in Social Movements*, edited by B. McLaughlin. New York: Free Press, 1969.

British National Council of Single Parents (London) newsletter, no. 4, April 1981.

Bryant, Nancy. "Self-Help Groups and Professionals—Cooperation or Conflict?" In *Helping One Another: Self-Help Groups in a Changing World*, edited by Alfred H. Katz and Eugene I. Bender. Oakland, Calif.: Third Party Publishers, 1990.

Cermak, Timmen. "Diagnostic Criteria for Co-dependency." *Journal of Psychoactive Drugs* 18 (1986).

Cermak, Timmen; Terry Hunt; Bonnie Keene; and Thomas W. "Co-dependency: More than a Catchword." *Patient Care*, 15 August 1989.

De Cocq, Gustave. "European and North American Self-Help Movements: Some Contrasts." In *Helping One Another: Self-Help-Groups in a Changing World*, edited by Alfred H. Katz and Eugene I. Bender. Oakland, Calif.: Third Party Publishers, 1990.

Eccles, John. "A Group for Mothers of the Mentally Retarded." *Australian Mental Retardation Digest* 12 (1981).

Emerick, Robert. "Self-Help Groups for Former Patients: Relations with Mental Health Professionals." *Hospital and Community Psychiatry* 41 (April 1990).

Gartner, Alan, and Frank Riessman. "Made for Each Other: Self-Help Groups and Mental Health Agencies." *Community Mental Health* 13 (1980).

Gussow, Zachary, and George Tracy. "Self-Help Health Groups: A Grass Roots Response to a Need for Services." *Journal of Applied Behavioral Science* 12 (September 1976).

Hatfield, Agnes. "The National Alliance for the Mentally Ill: A Decade Later." *Community Mental Health Journal* 27, no. 2 (1991).

———. "Self-Help Groups for Families of the Mentally Ill." *Social Work* 26 (1981).

Jacobs, Marion, and Gerald Goodman. "Psychology and Self-Help Groups: Predictions on a Partnership." *American Psychologist*, January 1989.

Katz, Alfred H. "Self-Help Groups and Professionals: General Issues." In *Self-Help: Concepts and Applications*, edited by Alfred H. Katz et al. Philadelphia: Charles Press, 1991.

———. "Self-Help Organizations and Volunteer Participation in Social Welfare." *Social Work* 15, no. 1 (1970).

Knight, Bob; Richard Wollert; Leon Levy; Cynthia Frame; and Valerie Padget. "Self-Help Groups: The Members' Perspective," *American Journal of Community Psychology* 8 (1980).

Kurtz, Linda. "Cooperation and Rivalry between Helping Professionals and Members of A.A." *Health and Social Work* 10 (Spring 1985).

Leventhal, Gerald; Kenneth Maton; Edward Madara; and Marisa Julien. "The Birth and Death of Self-Help Groups: An Ecological Perspective." In *Helping One Another: Self-Help Groups in a Changing World*, edited by Alfred H. Katz and Eugene I. Bender. Oakland, Calif.: Third Party Publishers, 1990.

Levy, Leon. "Self-Help Groups: Types and Psychological Processes." *Journal of Behavioral Science* 12 (September 1976).

_____. "Self-Help Groups Viewed by Mental Health Professionals." *American Journal of Community Psychology* 6 (August 1978).

Madara, Edward, and Camille Grish. "Finding Out More about How Self-Help Groups Help." *Network*, August–September 1981.

Maton, Kenneth; Gerald Leventhal; Edward Madara; and Marisa Julien. "The Birth and Death of Self-Help Groups: A Population Ecology Perspective." In *Helping One Another: Self-Help-Groups in a Changing World*, edited by Alfred H. Katz and Eugene I. Bender. Oakland, Calif.: Third Party Publishers, 1990.

Matzat, Jürgen. "Self-Help Groups in West Germany." *Acta Psychiatrica Scandinavia* 76 (1987).

Morantz, Regina. "19th Century Health Reform and Women: A Program of Self-Help." In *Medicine without Doctors*, edited by Günter Risse, Ronald Numbers, and Judith Leavitt. New York: Science History Publications, 1977.

Mullan, Fitzhugh. "Self-Help Groups and Public Health." Paper delivered at the symposium Self-Help and the Impact of Life-Threatening Conditions, Chicago, 1989.

Ogg, Elizabeth. "Partners in Coping." Public Affairs Pamphlet no. 559. New York: Public Affairs Committee, 1978.

Palmblad, Jan. "Stress and Immunological Competence: Studies in Man." In *Psychoneuroimmunology*, edited by Robert Ader, 229–57. New York: Academic Press, 1981.

Pilisuk, Marc. "Delivery of Social Support: The Social Inoculation." *American Journal of Orthopsychiatry* 52, no. 1 (1982).

Pinker, Roy. "An Alternative View." In *Social Workers: Their Role and Tasks*. London: Bedford Square Press, 1982.

Riger, Stephanie. "Vehicles for Empowerment: The Case of Feminist Movement Organizations." *Prevention in Human Services* 3 (1983–84).

Robinson, David. "The Self-Help Component of Primary Health Care." *Social Science and Medicine* 14a (January 1980).

Silverman, Phyllis, and Diane Smith. "Helping in Mutual Help Groups for the Physically Diasbled." In *The Self-Help Revolution*, edited by Alan Gartner and Frank Riessman. New York: Human Sciences Press, 1984.

Stewart, Miriam. "Expanding Theoretical Conceptualizations of Self-Help Groups." *Social Science and Medicine* 21, no. 9 (1990).

Toseland, Ronald, and Lynda Hacker. "Self-Help Groups and Professional Involvement." *Social Work* 27 (July 1982).

Weiss, Joan. "Genetic Support Groups: A Continuum of Genetic Services." *Women and Health* 15, no. 3 (1989).

Wollert, Richard; Leon Levy; and Bob Knight. "Help-Giving in Behavioral Control and Stress-Coping Self-Help Groups." *Small Group Behavior* 13 (1982).

Yoak, Margaret, and Mark Chesler. "Alternative Professional Roles in Health Care Delivery: Leadership Patterns in Self-Help Groups." *Journal of Applied Behavioral Science* 21, no. 4 (1985).

# Index

acquired immunodeficiency syndrome (AIDS), and self-help, 2, 9
Ader, Roger, 40
Adult Children of Alcoholics (ACA), 9, 42, 50-58; "The Problem," 52, 56-57; "The Solution," 56-57
Al-Anon Family Groups, 51-52, 53, 58, 111
Alateen, 51, 53, 58, 111
Alcoholics Anonymous, 1, 8, 10, 14, 20, 29-30, 37, 51, 53, 54, 55, 58, 59, 60, 61, 64, 65, 66, 67, 68, 71, 75, 80, 91, 104, 108, 110, 111; as the basis of 12-step groups, 9-14; "Big Book," 29; the Higher Power, 12, 13, 19, 57, 65, 68; and the Oxford Group, 10, 27; the 12 steps, 11, 12, 13, 20, 24, 26, 37, 54, 57, 67, 110; the 12 traditions, 12, 13, 20, 54, 61, 64, 91
Alinsky, Saul, 84
Alliance of Genetic Support Groups, 108-9
American Association of Retired Persons, 18
American Psychiatric Association, 46
American Psychological Association, 80
American Schizophrenic Association, 23
Americans with Disabilities Act (1990), 88, 90, 91

Association for Retarded Children, 14, 87, 94-95

Bandura, Albert, 31, 35, 36, 37, 38
Barath, Arpad, 99
Barry, Patricia, et al., 107
Belgium, self-help in, 2 96
Bender, Eugene I., 9, 105
bereavement, and self-help, 15, 16-18, 39-40
Black, Rita, 74
Blumer, Herbert, 108
Borman, Leonard, 72
British National Council of Single Parents, 23
Bryant, Nancy, 74
Bush, George, 88, 89

Cameron, William, 103-4
Canada, and self-help, 72, 96, 97-98, 100, 101
cancer patients, and self-help, 15-16, 23, 25, 28, 77, 99, 105
Candlelighters, 77, 111
Carter, Jimmy, 43
Centers for Disease Control, 94
cerebal palsy, and self-help, 14
Cermak, Timmen, 50, 51
Chesler, Mark, 25, 28, 77
Clinard, Marshall, 33-34

Cocaine Anonymous, 10, 57, 62
co-dependency, and self-help, 13, 50-53, 54, 55, 57
Co-Dependents Anonymous (CDA), 13, 57
cognitive restructuring, and self-help-group operations, 22-24, 31
The Compassionate Friends, 17
cooperative organizations (Great Britain), and history of self-help, 6

Darwin, Charles, 3
De Cocq, Gustave, 95-96
deinstitutionalization, 43, 48, 49
disabilities, persons with. *See* handicapped individuals
Dix, Dorothea, 42
Drachman, Diane, 74

Eastern-bloc countries, self-help in, 2
Economic Opportunity Act (1964), 85
Education for All Handicapped Act (1974), 87
Elwell, Rhonda, 54
Emerick, Robert, 73
empowerment, and self-help, 31, 35

Fisher, Robert, 85
40+ Club, 9, 111
Freud, Sigmund, 32, 42
Friendly Societies (Great Britain), and history of self-help, 5-6

Gamblers Anonymous, 10, 53
Gartner, Alan, 76
genetic disorders, and self-help, 14, 89, 94, 108-9, 110
Germany, and self-help, 2, 96, 98-99
Goodman, Gerald, 102
Goodwyn, Lawrence, 83, 84
Great Britain: history of self-help, 3-6; and national health care, 95; and self-help, 2, 23, 96, 100
Greenleaf, Jael, 52
Grish, Camille, 72
GROW, 73, 80, 111

Gussow, Zachary, 72

Hacker, Lynda, 72, 75
handicapped individuals, and self-help, 3, 8, 14, 15, 23-24, 46-47, 59, 60, 72-74, 87, 88, 91 100
Hatfield, Agnes, 23, 43, 44, 45, 49
health maintenance organizations (HMOs), 102
Hecker, George, 46
hemophilia, and self-help, 14, 24-25, 87, 108
Hughes, Harold, 91
human-services agencies, and self-help groups, 1, 70-71, 73; government agencies, 78-79, 103
human-services professionals, and self-help groups, 70-78, 79-82, 103

immigration, and early self-help (United States), 7-8

Jacobs, Marion, 102
Johnson, Hazle, 84, 85
Johnson, Lyndon B., 64-65

Kaminer, Wendy, 51
Kennedy, John F., 14, 93-94
Killian, Lewis, 104
Knight, Bob, et al., 25
Koop, C. Everett, 78-79, 94-95, 110
Kropotkin, Peter, 3-4
Kurtz, Linda, 75

Levy, Leon, 22-23, 24, 75
Lieber, Leonard, 72
Lieberman, Morton, 72
Living through Cancer, 16
Low, Abraham, 67, 72

Madara, Edward, 72
manic-depressive syndrome, and self-help, 23, 43, 61
Maslow, Abraham, "Hierarchy of Needs," 32-35, 37
Matzat, Jürgen, 98, 99
Mental Health Liaison Group, 46-47

Mental Health Systems Act (1980), 43
mentally ill individuals, and self-help, 2,
    23, 38, 42-50, 54, 58, 73, 75, 87,
    88, 93, 94, 102
mental retardation, and self-help, 14, 27-
    28, 87, 93-94
Mothers against Drunk Driving
    (MADD), 87, 111
Mullan, Fitzhugh, 86
muscular dystrophy, and self-help, 14
mutual aid, and the evolution of self-
    help, 3-8

Narcotics Anonymous, 10, 111
National Alliance for the Mentally Ill
    (NAMI), 23, 42-50, 58, 73, 88
National Association of Social Workers,
    80
National Commission on Mental Illness
    and Mental Retardation, 93
National Council of Independent Living
    Centers (NCILC), 88, 111
National Council on Self-Help and
    Public Health, 79
national health care: in the United States,
    89, 94; in Great Britain, 95
National Heart, Blood, and Lung
    Institute, 94
National Hemophilia Foundation, 14, 87
National Institute of Mental Health
    (NIMH), 45, 46, 47, 88, 94, 95
National Institutes of Health, 89, 95
National Marfan Foundation, 89
National Organization for Rare
    Disorders (NORD), 108
Netherlands, self-help in, 2 96

Overeaters Anonymous, 10, 13, 26, 53,
    111

Parents Anonymous, 10, 26, 66, 69, 72
Parents for Parents, 14-15
Parents without Partners, 68, 105, 111
personal disclosure, and self-help-group
    operations, 27-28
populism, and self-help, 82-91

public policy and self-help: in Canada,
    97-98; in Germany, 98-100; in
    Great Britain, 100; in the United
    States, 20-21, 87-90, 92-95, 100-
    102, 103, 110

Rational Recovery Systems, 13
Reagan, Ronald, 43, 44, 47, 94
Recovery, Inc., 67, 72, 73, 80, 106, 111
Riessman, Frank, 76
Riger, Stephanie, 68-69
Robinson, David, 29
Romeder, Jean-Marie, 72

Scandinavian countries, self-help in, 2
schizophrenia, and self-help, 23, 43, 44,
    45, 47, 48, 111
Secular Organization for Sobriety, 13
self-concept, 30-31
self-efficacy, 31, 37
self-esteem, 30-31
self-reliance, 30-31
SHARE, 15
Sheehan, Susan, 47
Silverman, Phyllis, 24, 28
Smith, Diane, 24, 28
Social Darwinism, 3
socialization, and self-help-group
    operations, 28-29
social-learning theories: and
    immunological competence, 38-
    41; role modeling, 35-36, self-
    efficacy, 37; social comparison,
    36-37; social support, 38;
    symbolic meaning, 37-38
Society of Americans for Recovery
    (SOAR), 91
Starr, Shirley, 45-46
Stewart, Miriam, 35, 39

THEOS, 18
Third World countries, and self-help, 3
Torrey, E. Fuller, 47, 48
Toseland, Ronald, 72, 75
Tracy, George, 72
trade unions (Great Britain), and history
    of self-help, 4-5

Turner, Ralph, 104
12 steps. *See* Alcoholics Anonymous
12 traditions. *See* Alcoholics
    Anonymous

U.S. Commission on Mental Health, 43
U.S. Department of Health and Human
    Services, 1

War on Poverty, 84
West, Cornel, 84

widows/widowers, and self-help, 17-18,
    20, 39, 40, 62, 68, 70
Wilson, Bill ("Bill W.," A.A. co-
    founder), 60
Woititz, Janet G., 52
Wollert, Richard, et al., 25, 26, 77
Workshop on Self-Help and Public
    Health (1987), 78, 95, 110
World Health Organization, 86, 100

Yoak, Margaret, 25, 28, 77

# The Author

Alfred H. Katz, professor emeritus at the UCLA Schools of Public Health and Social Welfare, received his M.A. from the University of New Zealand and his D.S.W. from Columbia University. He has been visiting professor at the London School of Economics, the Hebrew University in Jerusalem, and the Universities of Copenhagen and Aberdeen. A practitioner, administrator, and researcher in family, child welfare, and industrial and health social work for 15 years before assuming his UCLA academic position, he has been a consultant on self-help to the World Health Organization, the Ford Foundation, and a number of state and federal U.S. agencies. His books include *Parents of the Handicapped* (1961), *Health and the Community* (1965), *Hemophilia: A Study in Hope and Reality* (1970), *The Strength in US: Self-Help Groups in the Modern World* (1976, with Eugene I. Bender), *Self-Care: Lay Initiatives in Health* (1976, with Lowell Levin and Erik Holst), and *Helping One Another: Self-Help Groups in a Changing World* (1990, with Eugene I. Bender).